The Book of Avoidant Personality Disorder

Your Step-by-Step Guide for Thriving with AvPD

Lilian Nicole

TABLE OF CONTENTS.

INTRODUCTION.

Welcome to **"The Book of Avoidant Personality Disorder,"** a book dedicated to understanding and overcoming Avoidant Personality Disorder. If you're holding this book, chances are you or someone you care about is struggling with AvPD. Perhaps you've noticed persistent feelings of inadequacy, hypersensitivity to rejection, or a strong desire to avoid social interactions. These experiences can be incredibly challenging and may have a profound impact on various aspects of your life.

Overview of Avoidant Personality Disorder.

If you've ever felt an overwhelming fear of rejection, a deep- seated sense of inadequacy, or a strong desire to avoid social situations, you might be familiar with Avoidant Personality Disorder.

AvPD is a complex mental condition marked by a chronic pattern of social inhibition, feelings of inadequacy and hypersensitivity to criticism.

Imagine walking into a social gathering and feeling like everyone is judging you. You might worry about saying or doing the wrong thing for fear of being perceived negatively by others. These thoughts and feelings can be so distressing that you avoid all social interactions, despite your desire for connection and belonging.

People with AvPD often struggle to form and maintain personal and professional relationships. They may come across as shy, withdrawn, or reserved, giving the impression that they are aloof or disinterested. However, beneath this facade lies a deep-seated fear of rejection and humiliation, which can be paralyzing.

One of the main characteristics of AvPD is the avoidance of social situations due to fear of being judged negatively. This avoidance can present itself in a number of ways, including avoiding social gatherings, refraining from speaking up in meetings or classes, or avoiding activities that require interaction with others. While avoidance may bring short-term relief from anxiety, it can also reinforce feelings of isolation and loneliness.

Another symptom of AvPD is a continuous sense of inadequacy and low self-esteem. You might constantly doubt your abilities and worth, believing that you are inherently flawed or inferior to others. This poor self-image can be incredibly damaging, hurting your confidence and self-esteem in all aspects of life.

Avoidant Personality Disorder is a complicated and frequently misunderstood mental health condition. It is falls under the umbrella of Cluster C personality disorder, which is defined by anxious and fearful behavior. People struggling with AvPD typically exhibit a pervasive pattern of social restraint, feelings of inadequacy, and hypersensitivity to negative evaluation. These traits may significantly interfere with their ability to form and maintain relationships, pursue opportunities, and engage in social activities.

Individuals with AvPD often experience intense anxiety and fear in social situations, causing them to avoid such interactions whenever possible. This avoidance can extend to work, school, and other areas of life, limiting their ability to reach their full potential. Despite their desire for social connection, the fear of rejection and humiliation can overpower them, leading to isolation and loneliness.

Importance of Understanding and Addressing Avoidant Personality Disorder.

Understanding AvPD is crucial for several reasons. To begin, recognizing the symptoms and patterns of AvPD can help you in making sense of your feelings and experiences. It can be reassuring to know that there is a name for what you're going through and that you are not alone in your struggles.

Furthermore, understanding AvPD can pave the way to effective treatment and support. While AvPD can be challenging to overcome, you can manage its symptoms to improve your quality of life.

Therapy, particularly cognitive-behavioral therapy (CBT), can be highly effective in helping you challenge negative thought patterns, improve self-esteem, and develop healthier coping mechanisms.

Ultimately, addressing AvPD can lead to significant improvements in your relationships and overall well-being. You can improve your ability to form meaningful connections and achieve your goals by learning to manage your symptoms and participate more confidently in social situations.

In "The Book of Avoidant Personality Disorder", we will explore AvPD in depth, examining its causes, symptoms, and treatment options. We will also provide practical strategies to help you manage your symptoms and live a more fulfilling life. Whether you are personally affected by AvPD or supporting someone who is, this book aims to provide guidance, support, and hope on the path to recovery.

CHAPTER ONE.

Understanding Avoidant Personality Disorder.

If you're reading this, you're probably wondering what Avoidant Personality Disorder (AvPD) is and how it affects you or someone you care about.
Understanding AvPD is the first step toward managing its symptoms and improving your quality of life. Let's get into the details of AvPD, including its diagnostic criteria and classification, as well as prevalence and statistics.

What is Avoidant Personality Disorder (AvPD)?

Avoidant Personality Disorder (AvPD) is a mental health condition defined by a pattern of social inhibition, feelings of inadequacy, and hypersensitivity to negative evaluation. Individuals with AvPD often avoid social or occupational activities requiring significant interpersonal contact due to fear of judgment, rejection, or disapproval. This can have a substantial influence on their ability to form and sustain relationships, contributing to feelings of loneliness and isolation. It is important to remember that AvPD is a recognized mental health condition that should be diagnosed and treated by a qualified mental health practitioner. Therapy and, in certain situations, medications can help manage the symptoms of AvPD.

Diagnostic criteria and classification.

Understanding the diagnostic criteria and classification of Avoidant Personality Disorder (AvPD) can help you identify and seek help for your struggles. AvPD is classified as a Cluster C personality disorder in the Diagnostic and Statistical Manual of Mental Disorders (DSM-5), a diagnostic and classification tool used by mental health professionals.

Let's examine some of the criteria used to diagnose AvPD:

1. **Avoidance of Occupational Activities:** You may avoid jobs or activities that involve significant interpersonal contact out of fear of criticism, rejection,

or disapproval. This avoidance can hinder your career growth and limit your opportunities for advancement.

2. **Avoidance of Social Interactions:** You may avoid social interactions or situations where you might be evaluated or judged by others. This avoidance can lead to feelings of isolation and loneliness despite your desire for connection.

3. **Avoidance Due to Fear of Embarrassment:** You may avoid social or occupational activities due to fear of being embarrassed or humiliated. This fear can be so intense that it affects your ability to perform daily activities.

4. **Preoccupation with Being Criticized or Rejected:** You may be preoccupied with the concerns of being criticized, rejected, or ridiculed by others. This preoccupation can be overwhelming, leading to uneasiness in social situations.

5. **Inhibition in New Interpersonal situations:** You may feel inhibited or shy in new interpersonal situations, making it difficult for you to initiate or continue conversations. This inhibition can make it difficult to build new relationships or social bonds.

6. **Feelings of Inadequacy:** You may experience a pervasive sense of inadequacy and inferiority, which leads to low self-esteem. These feelings of inadequacy can affect many aspects of your life, including work, relationships, and self-image.

7. **Reluctance to Take Personal Risks:** You may be hesitant to take personal risks or participate in new activities for fear of failure or rejection. This reluctance may limit your opportunities for personal growth and development.

8. **Avoidance Interferes with Functioning:** Your avoidance behaviors have a substantial impact on your daily functioning and relationships. These behaviors may prevent you from achieving your goals or engaging in activities that are important to you.

9. **Onset in Early Adulthood:** The avoidance pattern usually begins in early adulthood and remains constant over time. You may have had AvPD symptoms since childhood or early adulthood, though their severity may vary.

10. **Not Better Explained by Another Mental Disorder:** Your symptoms cannot be better explained by another mental health disorder, such as Social Anxiety Disorder or Schizoid Personality Disorder. A thorough

assessment by a mental health specialist is required to distinguish AvPD from other disorders.

These criteria reflect the core features of AvPD and are used by mental health professionals to diagnose the disorder. If you identify with these criteria, it is important to seek support from a mental health expert who can do a thorough assessment and recommend appropriate treatment options.

Prevalence and Statistics.

Understanding the prevalence and statistics of Avoidant Personality Disorder (AvPD) can provide valuable insights into how common this disorder is and its impacts on individuals like you. While AvPD is less studied compared to other personality disorders, research has provided some estimates of its prevalence and impact on different groups of people.

Prevalence of Avoidant Personality Disorder.

AvPD is estimated to affect approximately 2.4% of the general population. This means that 2 to 3 people out of 100 may meet the AvPD diagnosis criteria. While this prevalence may seem low in comparison to other mental health conditions, it is important to remember that AvPD can have a major effect on the lives of those affected by it.

Gender Differences.

AvPD is diagnosed more often in women than in men. According to certain research, women are twice as likely to be diagnosed with AvPD compared to men. However, it is important to note that these gender differences might be influenced by various factors, including differences in help-seeking behavior and diagnostic practices.

Age of onset.

AvPD symptoms often appear in early adulthood, with the majority of people experiencing them by their late teens or early twenties. However, the exact age of onset varies by individual, and some may not seek help or receive a diagnosis until later in life.

People with AvPD often have co-occurring mental health conditions, such as depression, anxiety disorders, or other personality disorders. These co-occurring conditions can further complicate the diagnosis and treatment of AvPD.

Developmental Factors and Causes.

Understanding the developmental factors and causes of Avoidant Personality Disorder (AvPD) can provide valuable insights into why you or someone you care about are experiencing this challenging condition. While the exact causes of AvPD are not fully understood, research suggests that genetic, environmental, and psychological factors may contribute to its development.

Genetic Factors:

Genetic factors may influence the development of AvPD. According to studies, individuals with a family history of personality disorders, particularly Cluster C disorders such as AvPD, are more likely to develop the disorder themselves. However, genetics alone are insufficient to develop AvPD; other factors are most likely involved.

Environmental Factors:

Environmental factors, such as as early life experiences, can also contribute to the development of AvPD. Children who grow up in environments where they feel consistently rejected, criticized, or humiliated may develop a fear of social interactions and a sense of inferiority. Furthermore, traumatic experiences, such as bullying or abuse, can aggravate these feelings and contribute to the development of AvPD.

Psychological Factors:

Psychological factors, including personality traits and coping techniques, can also influence the development of AvPD. Individuals who are inherently timid or introverted, for example, may be more prone to developing AvPD, especially if they are subjected to significant stress or trauma. Additionally, individuals who struggle with emotion regulation or stress management may be more susceptible to develop AvPD as a coping mechanism for feelings of inadequacy and fear.

Attachment Theory:

Attachment theory suggests that the quality of early attachment relationships, particularly with primary caregivers, can influence the development of personality traits and coping mechanisms. Children
who experience inconsistent or unresponsive caregiving may develop insecure attachment styles, which can lead to feelings of fear and mistrust in relationships. These early attachment patterns can persist into adulthood and contribute to the development of AvPD.

Cognitive Factors:

Negative self-beliefs and distorted thinking patterns are two cognitive factors that can also contribute to the development of AvPD. Individuals with AvPD, for example, may interpret neutral or positive social cues negatively, resulting in increased feelings of rejection and avoidance. Furthermore, they may hold rigid beliefs about themselves and others, which makes it difficult for them to build and sustain good relationships.

Social Learning:

According to social learning theory, individuals might learn avoidant behaviors by observing others, particularly their parents or caregivers. If a child sees that avoidance is an efficient way to deal with social situations, they may adopt similar behaviors.

Biological factors:

According to some research, biological factors such as differences in brain structure or function may play a role in the development of AvPD. However, more research is needed to fully understand the role of biology in AvPD.

Temperamental Factors:

Temperament refers to a person's natural behavioral patterns. Some people may be born with a disposition that makes them more sensitive to rejection or criticism, which increases their chances of developing AvPD.

Cultural Factors:

Societal norms and expectations can influence the development of AvPD. Individuals in cultures that place a strong emphasis on social conformity and avoiding conflict may be more likely to develop avoidant behaviors.

Life Events and Stressors:

Significant losses, traumas, or major life changes can trigger or worsen symptoms of AvPD. These events can exacerbate feelings of insecurity and lead to increased avoidance behaviors.

Personality traits:

Certain personality traits, such as introversion, neuroticism, or a proclivity to avoid danger, may be linked to an increased risk of developing AvPD. These traits can contribute to a pattern of avoidance and social withdrawal.

Parenting Style:

The parenting style of caregivers can influence the development of AvPD. Overly critical, controlling, or rejecting parenting styles can lead to feelings of inadequacy and fear of rejection in children.

Social and Cultural Factors:

The development of AvPD can be influenced by societal pressures, cultural expectations, and social conventions.

Individuals in cultures that place a high value on individual achievement and success, for example, may feel driven to avoid social interactions that could result in failure or rejection.

These factors interact in complex ways, contributing to the development of AvPD. Understanding these aspects can provide insight into the problem, but it is important to remember that AvPD is a complex condition with no clear explanation. Treatment typically involves a combination of therapy, medication and support to help individuals manage their symptoms and improve their quality of life.

Co-morbidity with other Disorders.

Understanding the relationship between Avoidant Personality Disorder (AvPD) and other mental health problems might help you better grasp its intricacies and impact on your general well-being.

AvPD is often associated with other disorders, a phenomenon known as comorbidity. Let's explore some of the most prevalent comorbidities of AvPD and how they affect you.

Social Anxiety Disorder (SAD):

One of the most common AvPD comorbidities is Social Anxiety Disorder (SAD). SAD is defined by acute fear or anxiety about social situations, which often leads to avoidance of certain situations. You may find yourself overly worried about embarrassing yourself or being judged negatively by others. This fear can be so overwhelming that it limits your ability to engage in social activities or form meaningful relationships.

Depression:

Depression is another common comorbidity of AvPD. The constant feelings of inadequacy, rejection, and isolation associated with AvPD can have a negative impact on your mental health and cause depressive symptoms. You may experience chronic sadness, hopelessness, and worthlessness, making it difficult to find joy in activities you once enjoyed.

Other Personality disorders:

AvPD is often linked with other personality disorders, particularly Cluster C disorders like Dependent Personality Disorder and Obsessive-Compulsive Disorder. These disorders share similar features such as anxiety, fearfulness, and a need for control or reassurance, which may contribute to their co-occurrence.

Substance Use Disorders:

Individuals with AvPD are also more likely to have substance use issues. You may turn to alcohol or drugs to cope with the overpowering feelings of worry, depression, or inadequacy caused by AvPD. However, substance abuse can worsen your symptoms and cause additional problems in your life.

Eating Disorders:

Eating disorders such as Anorexia Nervosa and Bulimia Nervosa tend to coincide with AvPD. You may use food or eating behaviors to cope with feelings of inadequacy or to regain control over your life. However, these activities can be detrimental to both your physical and mental health.

Post-traumatic Stress Disorder (PTSD):

If you have a history of trauma or abuse, you may be at higher risk of developing PTSD, which can coexist with AvPD.

Traumatic experiences can heighten your feelings of fear, anxiety, and avoidance, making it difficult for you to function in everyday life.

Generalized Anxiety Disorder (GAD):

GAD is defined by excessive worry and anxiety about a various aspects of life, including work, relationships, and health. Individuals with AvPD may also experience GAD, as they often experience heightened anxiety and worry, particularly in social situations.

Panic Disorder:

Panic disorder is defined by recurring panic attacks, which are sudden and intense episodes of fear or discomfort. Individuals with AvPD may be more prone to panic attacks, especially when they feel exposed or vulnerable.

Obsessive-Compulsive Disorder (OCD):

OCD is defined by intrusive thoughts (obsessions) and repetitive behaviors (compulsions) that are performed to relieve anxiety. Individuals with AvPD may exhibit obsessive-compulsive traits, such as a desire for order or perfectionism, which can overlap with OCD symptoms.

Borderline Personality Disorder (BPD):

BPD is defined by instability in relationships, self-image, and emotions. While BPD and AvPD are distinct disorders, they can co-occur, particularly due to shared features such as fear of abandonment and interpersonal difficulties.

Dependent Personality Disorder (DPD):

Dependent Personality Disorder is defined by a pervasive and excessive need to be cared for, which can lead to submissive and clingy behavior. Individuals with AvPD may exhibit dependent traits, as they may seek reassurance and validation from others to alleviate feelings of inadequacy.

Avoidant Behavior in Other Disorders:

Avoidant behavior is not exclusive to AvPD; it can also be present in other mental health disorders, such as PTSD, where avoidance is a common symptom. Individuals with PTSD may avoid situations or stimuli that remind them of traumatic events, similar to how individuals with AvPD avoid social interactions.

Mood Disorders:

Major depressive disorder or dysthymia are often comorbid with AvPD. The persistent feelings of inadequacy and rejection associated with AvPD can contribute to the emergence of depressive symptoms.

Chronic Pain conditions:

Due to the interplay between psychological and physical health, individuals with AvPD may be more susceptible to developing chronic pain conditions such as fibromyalgia or chronic fatigue syndrome.

These comorbidities can complicate the diagnosis and treatment of AvPD, highlighting the importance of a comprehensive assessment by a mental health professional to address all aspects of your mental health.

CHAPTER TWO.

The Developmental Roots of AvPD.

Childhood Experiences and Attachment Theory.

Our childhood experiences play a major role in influencing who we are today. Understanding the impact of early life experiences on Avoidant Personality disorder (AvPD) is key to unraveling the developmental roots of this complex disorder. Let's explore how childhood experiences, particularly those related to attachment theory, can contribute to the development of AvPD.

Attachment Theory:

Attachment theory, proposed by psychologist John Bowlby, suggests that the early bonds we form with our caregivers profoundly influence our emotional and social development. According to this theory, children develop different attachment styles based on their interactions with caregivers, which can have long-lasting effects on their relationships and mental health.

For individuals with AvPD, childhood experiences often involve insecure attachment patterns. Insecure attachment is characterized by a lack of trust and security in relationships, which can stem from inconsistent or neglectful caregiving. Insecure attachment can cause children to feel undeserving of love and support, leading to the avoidance of close relationships in life.

The internal working model is a key aspect of the attachment theory. This model is developed during childhood and serves as a guide for how we perceive ourselves and others in relationships. Individuals with AvPD may have a negative internal working model, making it difficult to build and maintain close relationships.

Childhood Trauma:

Childhood trauma is another factor in the development of AvPD. Traumatic experiences, such as abuse, neglect, or loss, can have a significant impact on a child's development and contribute to AvPD later in life. Trauma can disrupt the formation of secure attachments and make it difficult to trust others, both of which are core features of AvPD.

Parenting Styles:

Parenting styles also influence the development of AvPD. Authoritarian or overprotective parenting can contribute to the development of avoidant tendencies in children, who may learn to avoid emotional expression or close relationships in order to avoid conflict or criticism. Neglectful parenting, on the other hand, might lead to AvPD as children may learn to self-isolate themselves in the absence of emotional support.

In conclusion, childhood experiences, particularly those related to attachment theory, play a significant role in the development of Avoidant Personality Disorder. Understanding how early life experiences influence our emotional and social development allows us to gain insight into the developmental roots of AvPD and strive toward more effective strategies for prevention and treatment.

Genetic and Environmental Influences.

Understanding Avoidant Personality Disorder (AvPD) requires taking into account both hereditary and environmental influences. These factors can interact in intricate ways, shaping our development and increasing our risks of developing AvPD. Let's examine at how genetics and our environment influence the development of this disorder, and what that implies for you.

Genetics plays a significant role in the development of AvPD. AvPD tends to run in families, indicating that there may be a genetic predisposition to the disorder. If a close family, such as a parent or sibling, has AvPD, you may be more likely to develop the condition yourself. However, having a genetic susceptibility does not guarantee that you will develop AvPD; environmental factors also play an important role.

Environmental factors, such as childhood experiences and parenting practices, can potentially influence the development of AvPD. Growing up in an unsupportive or judgmental environment, for example, can increase your risk of developing avoidant behaviors. Similarly, childhood trauma or neglect can contribute to the development of AvPD later in life.

The interaction between genetics and environment must also be considered. While genetics can increase your risk of developing AvPD, environmental factors can either accentuate or reduce that risk. For example, if you have a genetic tendency to AvPD but are raised in a loving and nurturing environment, you may be less likely to develop the disorder. On the other hand, if you have a genetic predisposition and have experienced major stress or neglect, your likelihood of developing AvPD may be higher.

It's also worth noting that genetic and environmental factors can interact in complex ways. For example, certain genetic factors may make you more sensitive to environmental stressors, increasing your likelihood of developing AvPD in response to adverse experiences. Understanding these interactions will enable us to better understand the development of AvPD and tailor interventions to address both genetic and environmental influences.

In conclusion, both genetic and environmental factors play a crucial role in the development of avoidant personality disorder. While genetics can increase your probability of developing the disorder, environmental factors can either amplify or mitigate that risk. Understanding how these factors interact enables us to gain insight into the developmental roots of AvPD and work toward more effective preventive and treatment measures.

Impact of Early Trauma and Rejection.

Early childhood experiences can have a profound impact on our development, especially when it comes to Avoidant Personality Disorder (AvPD). Childhood trauma and rejection can affect our beliefs about ourselves and others, contributing to the development of AvPD. Let's examine how early trauma and rejection affect the development of AvPD, and what that means for you.

Childhood trauma and rejection can have a long-lasting effect on our mental health and wellbeing. For individuals with AvPD, these experiences can be particularly impactful on their thoughts about themselves and others. If you have experienced trauma or rejection during your early years, it is crucial to recognize how these experiences may have influenced your development and led to the development of AvPD.

One of the key ways in which trauma and rejection can impact the development of AvPD is through the development of negative self-beliefs. Children who are traumatized or rejected may internalize their experiences, leading to feelings of worthlessness or inadequacy. These negative self-beliefs can last until adulthood, contributing to the avoidant behaviors associated with AvPD.

Early trauma and rejection can also impact our ability to trust others. Children who have experienced trauma or rejection may learn to be wary of others and avoid forming close relationships for fear of being hurt. This can contribute to the social isolation and avoidance of social situations seen in individuals with AvPD.

It's important to note that not everyone who experiences early trauma or rejection will develop AvPD. However, these experiences can increase the risk, especially when combined with other genetic or environmental factors. If you have experienced trauma or rejection as a child, it is essential that you seek support and therapy to address any negative thoughts or patterns of behavior that may have developed as a result.

In conclusion, the impact of early trauma and rejection on the development of Avoidant Personality Disorder cannot be understated. These experiences can affect our perceptions about ourselves and others, leading to the development of avoidant behaviors and social isolation that are characteristics of AvPD. If you experienced trauma or rejection as a child, it is crucial to seek support and therapy to address any lingering effects and work toward healing and recovery.

CHAPTER THREE.

Symptoms and Manifestations of AvPD.

Social Withdrawal and Isolation.

One of the hallmark symptoms of Avoidant Personality Disorder (AvPD) is social withdrawal and isolation. If you are living with AvPD, you may find yourself voiding social settings, feeling uncomfortable or anxious around others, and finding it challenging to build close relationships. Let's examine more closely, these AvPD symptoms and manifestations, as well as what they mean to you.

Social withdrawal is a common behavior amongst individuals with AvPD. You may avoid social gatherings, such as parties or meetings, out of fear of criticism or rejection. Even everyday interactions, such as walking to the grocery store or answering the phone, can be overwhelming and anxiety-provoking. This avoidance can progress to social isolation, where you spend most of your time alone, in order to avoid contact with people.

Isolation goes beyond the physical avoidance of social interactions. It can also manifest as emotional withdrawal, where you keep your thoughts and feelings to yourself for fear of being rejected or criticized. This can make it difficult to build intimate relationships since you may be hesitant to open up to others or allow them to know the real you.

Social withdrawal and isolation can have a significant impact on your life. You may feel lonely and isolated, yearning for connection yet unsure how to overcome your fears and insecurities. This can lead to feelings of sadness, depression, and low self-esteem, further reinforcing your avoidant behaviors.

It's important to understand that social withdrawal and isolation are coping mechanisms for dealing with underlying fears and insecurities. You may believe that avoiding social situations protects you from rejection or criticism. However, this avoidance can hinder you from forming meaningful connections and benefiting from the support and companionship that healthy relationships provide.

If you are struggling with social withdrawal and isolation due to AvPD, it is essential to seek assistance and therapy. Therapy can help you in identifying the root causes of your avoidant behaviors and developing strategies to overcome them. You can learn to challenge negative beliefs about yourself and others, practice social skills, and progressively expose yourself to social situations in a supportive environment.

Hypersensitivity to criticism and rejection.

Living with Avoidant Personality Disorder (AvPD) can be difficult, especially when it comes to criticism and rejection. If you have AvPD, you may find yourself highly sensitive to criticism, fearful of rejection in social situations, and going to great lengths to avoid situations where you might be judged. Let's examine more closely these AvPD symptoms and manifestations, as well as what they mean for you.

AvPD is characterized by a heightened sensitivity to criticism. Even mild or constructive criticism might feel like a personal attack, leaving you upset, defensive, or embarrassed. This hypersensitivity can make it difficult to receive feedback or constructive criticism in a healthy way because you may interpret it as confirmation of your fears of being unworthy or inadequate.

Similarly, fear of rejection can drive avoidant behaviors in AvPD. You may avoid social events or interactions entirely, fearing that others would reject or abandon you if they get to know the real you. This fear can create a self-fulfilling prophecy, whereby your avoidance behaviors increase the likelihood of rejection, reinforcing your fears.

Hypersensitivity to criticism and rejection can be profound. You may find yourself avoiding social encounters or opportunities for personal growth, limiting your potential and hindering your ability to form meaningful connections with others. This might result in feelings of loneliness, low self-esteem, and a sense of being misunderstood or unappreciated.

It is important to recognize that hypersensitivity to criticism and rejection are common symptoms of AvPD and are not a reflection of your worth or value as a person. Therapy can be extremely beneficial in addressing these symptoms, as well as in developing healthy coping strategies for criticism and rejection. You can learn to challenge your negative self-beliefs, become more resilient to criticism, and nurture self-compassion and acceptance.

Fear of Disapproval and Negative Evaluation.

Living with Avoidant Personality Disorder (AvPD) can mean constantly fearing disapproval and negative evaluation from others. If you have AvPD, you may be highly sensitive to other people's judgments, going to great lengths to avoid situations in which you might be judged, and experiencing intense anxiety over being criticized or rejected. Let's examine more closely these AvPD symptoms and manifestations, as well as what they mean to you.

Fear of disapproval is a common symptom of AvPD. You may find yourself constantly seeking reassurance or acceptance from others, fearing that you will be judged or criticized if you make a mistake or express your true thoughts and feelings. This fear can be paralyzing, making it difficult to take risks or assert yourself in social situations.

Similarly, in AvPD, fear of negative evaluation can lead to avoidant behaviors. You may avoid social events or interactions where you are concerned about being poorly appraised or criticized. This can involve not speaking up in meetings, avoiding social gatherings, or avoiding situations where you may be in the spotlight.

The impact of fear of disapproval and negative evaluation can be significant. You may find yourself holding back in social situations, scared to be yourself or express your thoughts for fear of being judged. This might cause emotions of loneliness, isolation, and a sense of being misunderstood or underappreciated.

It is important to recognize that fear of disapproval and negative evaluation are symptoms of AvPD and do not reflect your personal worth or value. Therapy can be extremely beneficial in addressing these symptoms, boosting confidence and self-esteem, and learning healthy ways to cope with criticism and rejection.

Avoidance of Intimate Relationships and Social Activities.

Avoidant Personality Disorder (AvPD) can lead to a strong aversion to intimate relationships and social activities. If you're living with AvPD, you might find yourself avoiding close relationships, feeling uncomfortable in social settings, and preferring solitude over social interactions. Let's explore these symptoms and manifestations of AvPD in more detail and what they mean for you.

Avoidance of intimate relationships is a common feature of AvPD. You might find yourself avoiding romantic relationships or maintaining superficial relationships to avoid the risk of rejection or criticism. Even in existing relationships, you might struggle to fully open up and express your true thoughts and feelings, fearing that you will be judged or rejected if you do.

Similarly, avoidance of social activities can be a prominent symptom of AvPD. You might find yourself avoiding social gatherings, parties, or other events where you might be expected to interact with others. This avoidance can be driven by a fear of being judged, criticized, or rejected by others, leading you to prefer solitude over social interactions.

The impact of avoidance of intimate relationships and social activities can be profound. You may feel isolated and lonely, longing for connection but unsure how to overcome your fears and insecurities. This can lead to feelings of sadness, depression, and low self-esteem, further reinforcing your avoidant behaviors.

It's important to recognize that avoidance of intimate relationships and social activities are common symptoms of AvPD and are not a reflection of your worth or value as a person. Therapy can be incredibly helpful in addressing these symptoms, helping you build confidence in social situations and learn healthy ways to form and maintain intimate relationships.

In conclusion, avoidance of intimate relationships and social activities are common symptoms of Avoidant Personality Disorder. If you're dealing with AvPD, you might find yourself avoiding close relationships and social interactions, preferring solitude over social activities. It's important to seek support and therapy to address these symptoms and work towards building meaningful connections with others. Remember, you are not alone, and help is available to support you on your journey to healing and recovery.

CHAPTER FOUR.

Psychological Mechanisms and Patterns.

Core Beliefs and Cognitive Distortions.

Living with Avoidant Personality Disorder (AvPD) could mean grappling with deeply ingrained core beliefs and cognitive distortions that shape how you see yourself and the world around you. These beliefs and distortions can have a major impact on AvPD symptoms and behaviors. Let's explore these psychological mechanisms and patterns, and what they mean for you.

Core beliefs constitute fundamental beliefs about ourselves, others, and the world around us. Individuals with AvPD often harbor basic beliefs around themes of worthlessness, unlovability, and inadequacy. You might believe that you are innately imperfect or unworthy of love and acceptance, therefore you avoid situations where these beliefs are challenged.

Cognitive distortions are exaggerated or irrational thought patterns that can contribute to undesirable feelings and behaviors.

Here are some common cognitive distortions that people commonly experience:

1. **All-or-nothing thinking (also known as dichotomous thinking):** This is when you see things in black and white without considering any shades of grey. For example, believing that if you aren't perfect, then you're a failure.

2. **Overgeneralization:** Drawing broad conclusions from limited evidence or a single negative experience. For example, if one date does not go well, you may assume that you will never find a compatible partner.

3. **Mental filtering:** Concentrating solely on the negative aspects of a situation and disregarding or discounting the positive parts. For example, dismissing compliments and dwelling only on criticism.

4. **Disqualifying the positive:** Viewing pleasant experiences or accomplishments as irrelevant or insignificant. For example, believing that your achievement is solely due to luck and failing to recognize your own abilities.

5. **Jumping to conclusions:** Making assumptions without adequate proof. This can involve mind-reading (assuming you know what others are thinking) and fortune-telling (predicting unpleasant outcomes without evidence).

6. **Catastrophizing:** Exaggerating the significance or repercussions of an event while assuming the worst possible outcome. For example, believing that a slight error at work will result in immediate termination.

7. **Personalization:** Taking too much personal responsibility for events or situations beyond your control. Blaming yourself for things that are not your fault.

8. **Emotional reasoning:** Believing that your feelings reflect reality even when there is little or no evidence to support it. For example, being nervous about a forthcoming event and assuming that it would undoubtedly be a disaster.

9. **Should statements:** Using "should," "must," or "ought to" expressions to put strict expectations on yourself or others. For example, thinking "I should always be able to handle everything on my own."

10. **Labeling:** Assigning global, negative labels to oneself or others based on specific behaviors or mistakes. For example, labeling yourself a "failure" because of a single setback.

It's important to recognize that these cognitive distortions are common and many people experience them from time to time. However, when they become persistent and contribute to distress or impaired functioning, cognitive restructuring can be beneficial.

It is essential to identify these core beliefs and cognitive distortions in order to challenge and change them. Therapy can be quite effective in identifying and addressing these beliefs, helping you to develop more adaptive ways of thinking and behaving. You can learn to challenge negative beliefs, reframe irrational thoughts, and develop a more balanced and realistic view of yourself and the world around you.

Finally, core beliefs and cognitive distortions play a significant role in the development and maintenance of Avoidant Personality Disorder. If you are living with AvPD, you may find yourself dealing with deeply ingrained feelings of worthlessness and unlovability, as well as distorted thought patterns that contribute to negative emotions and behaviors. It is important to seek help and therapy to address these psychological mechanisms and work toward a more positive and realistic self-image.

Avoidance Strategies and Coping Mechanisms.

Avoidant Personality Disorder (AvPD) is often characterized by the use of avoidance strategies and coping mechanisms to deal with challenging situations and emotions. If you're living with AvPD, you might find yourself relying on these strategies to manage your fears and insecurities.

Here are some of the common avoidance strategies and coping mechanisms in AvPD and what they mean for you:

- One of the most common avoidance strategies in AvPD is social avoidance. You might avoid social situations or interactions where you fear you might be judged, criticized, or rejected by others. This can include avoiding parties, gatherings, or other events where you might be expected to interact with others, as well as avoiding close relationships where you fear you might be hurt or abandoned.

- Another common avoidance strategy is avoidance of risk and change. You might prefer to stick to familiar routines and environments, avoiding new experiences or opportunities for personal growth. This can lead to a sense of stagnation and missed opportunities for growth and development.

- Coping mechanisms in AvPD often revolve around maintaining a sense of control and predictability. For example, you might engage in perfectionistic behaviors, striving to meet impossibly high standards in order to avoid criticism or disapproval. You might also engage in self-criticism, constantly berating yourself for perceived shortcomings in order to avoid the pain of rejection or failure.

- Avoidance of emotions is another common coping mechanism in AvPD. You might find yourself suppressing or denying your emotions, fearing that expressing them will make you vulnerable to criticism or rejection. This can lead to a sense of emotional numbness and detachment from your own feelings.

While these avoidance strategies and coping mechanisms may provide temporary relief from your fears and insecurities, they can also contribute to the maintenance of AvPD symptoms and behaviors. Therapy can be incredibly helpful in identifying these patterns and developing more adaptive ways of coping. You can learn to challenge your avoidance behaviors, develop healthier coping mechanisms, and build resilience in the face of challenging situations.

In conclusion, avoidance strategies and coping mechanisms play a significant role in the experience of AvPD. If you're living with AvPD, you might find yourself relying on these strategies to manage your fears and insecurities. It's important to seek support and therapy to address these patterns and develop more adaptive ways of coping.

Emotional Regulation and Expression.

Emotional regulation and expression can be particularly challenging for those with Avoidant Personality Disorder (AvPD). If you're living with AvPD, you might find yourself struggling to manage your emotions, often feeling overwhelmed or unable to express them in a healthy way. Listed below are the complexities of emotional regulation and expression in AvPD and what they mean for you.

- One of the key challenges in AvPD is difficulty in recognizing and labeling emotions. You might find yourself feeling a mix of emotions but struggle to identify what you're feeling or why. This can lead to a sense of confusion and frustration, as you may not know how to effectively address or communicate your emotions to others.

- Another challenge is regulating intense emotions. Individuals with AvPD may experience emotions more intensely than others, leading to feelings of overwhelm or distress. You might find yourself struggling to cope with these intense emotions, often resorting to avoidance or suppression as a way to cope.

- Avoidance is a common coping mechanism in AvPD, particularly when it comes to managing emotions. You might avoid situations or people that trigger strong emotions, preferring to keep your emotions bottled up rather than risk expressing them and facing potential rejection or criticism.

- Additionally, individuals with AvPD may struggle with emotional expression, finding it difficult to express their feelings in a healthy and constructive way. You might fear that expressing your emotions will make you vulnerable or that others will see you as weak, leading you to suppress or deny your feelings.

It's important to recognize that emotional regulation and expression are skills that can be learned and improved with practice. Therapy can be incredibly helpful in developing these skills, helping you learn to identify and label your emotions, regulate intense emotions, and express your feelings in a healthy and constructive way.

In conclusion, emotional regulation and expression can be challenging for those with Avoidant Personality Disorder. If you're living with AvPD, you might find yourself struggling to manage your emotions, often resorting to avoidance or suppression as a way to cope. It's important to seek support and therapy to develop these skills and learn healthier ways of managing your emotions. Remember, you are not alone, and help is available to support you on your journey to healing and recovery.

CHAPTER FIVE.

Diagnosis and Assessment.

Screening tools and diagnostic procedures play a crucial role in identifying and diagnosing Avoidant Personality Disorder (AvPD). These tools help mental health professionals with assessing symptoms and determining if an individual meets the criteria for AvPD. Here, we will discuss some of the screening tools and diagnostic procedures that are commonly used in the assessment AvPD.

1. **Structured Clinical Interview for DSM-5 (SCID-5):** The SCID-5 is a semi-structured interview designed to assess various mental disorders, including AvPD. It consists of a series of questions based on the DSM-5 criteria for AvPD, allowing clinicians to evaluate symptoms and make an accurate diagnosis.

2. **Millon Clinical Multiaxial Inventory-IV (MCMI-IV):** The MCMI-IV is a self-report questionnaire that assesses a variety of personality traits and disorders, including AvPD. It provides clinicians with information about an

individual's personality structure and can help diagnose AvPD.

3. **Personality Assessment Inventory (PAI):** The PAI is another self-report questionnaire for assessing personality traits and psychopathology. It includes scales to help identify AvPD symptoms such as social isolation and hypersensitivity to criticism.

4. **Structured Interview for DSM-IV Personality (SIDP-IV):** Although designed for DSM-IV, the SIDP-IV is still used in clinical practice. It is a comprehensive interview that assesses for all personality disorders, including AvPD, by examining various aspects of personality functioning.

5. **International Personality Disorder Examination (IPDE):** The IPDE is a semi-structured interview that is designed to assess for personality disorders, including AvPD. It covers a range of AvPD-related criteria, including avoidance of social interactions and feelings of inadequacy.

6. **Avoidant Personality Disorder Severity Index (AVPDSI):** The AVPDSI is a self-report questionnaire for determining the severity of AvPD symptoms. It covers topics about avoidance behavior, social anxiety, and sensitive to criticism.

7. **Avoidant Personality Disorder Scale (APDS):** The APDS is a self-report questionnaire used to assess specific symptoms of AvPD. It includes items related to fear of rejection, reluctance to participate in social activities, and feelings of inadequacy.

8. **Clinical Assessment of Avoidant Personality Disorder (CAAP):** The CAAP is a structured interview that assesses AvPD symptoms using DSM-5 criteria. It includes questions about avoidance behavior, social anxiety, and interpersonal relationships.

9. **Minnesota Multiphasic Personality Inventory-2 (MMPI-2):** The MMPI-2 is a widely used self-report questionnaire that assesses a variety of personality traits and psychopathology. It can provide valuable information about a person's personality structure and identify potential features of AvPD.

10. **Beck Depression Inventory (BDI):** While not specific to personality disorders, the BDI is a self-report questionnaire designed to assess the severity of depressive symptoms. Depression often co-occurs with AvPD, so assessing for depressive symptoms is of the utmost importance in a comprehensive evaluation.

11. Hamilton Anxiety Rating Scale (HAM-A): Anxiety is a common co-occurring condition with AvPD. The HAM-A is a clinician-rated scale for assessing the intensity of anxiety symptoms, which can help in the diagnosis and management of AvPD.

12. Clinical interviews and observations: In addition to standardized assessments, clinicians often rely on clinical interviews and observations to diagnose AvPD. These interviews enable clinicians to gather information on a patient's symptoms, behaviors, and interpersonal functioning, all of which are essential for an accurate diagnosis.

13. Collateral information: Information from family members, friends, or other sources can also be useful in diagnosing AvPD. These individuals can provide extra information about the individual's behavior and symptoms, helping clinicians to come up with a more accurate diagnosis.

These screening tools and diagnostic procedures can help clinicians in assessing for AvPD and making an accurate diagnosis. They provide valuable information regarding an individual's symptoms and can help guide treatment planning to address the specific needs of individuals with AvPD.

Differential Diagnosis and Common Misdiagnosis.

Diagnosing Avoidant Personality Disorder (AvPD) can be challenging due to overlapping symptoms with other mental health conditions. It is important for clinicians to evaluate various differential diagnoses and be aware of common misdiagnosis. Here, we will explore conditions that are often confused with AvPD and how they differ.

1. **Social Anxiety Disorder (SAD):** Social Anxiety Disorder, shares similarities with AvPD, such as a fear of embarrassment and avoidance of social interactions. However, SAD is primarily defined by intense fear or anxiety in social situations, whereas AvPD is more about a deep-seated fear of rejection and criticism.

2. **Generalized Anxiety Disorder (GAD):** GAD is characterized by excessive worry and anxiety about various aspects of life, especially social interactions. Individuals with AvPD may experience anxiety, but it is usually more focused on social settings and interpersonal relationships rather than general circumstances.

3. **Dependent Personality Disorder (DPD):** DPD is distinguished by a strong urge to be cared for and a fear of separation. While individuals with AvPD may struggle with dependency issues, the core feature of AvPD is a fear of rejection and criticism, rather than a fear of being alone or without support.

4. **Obsessive-compulsive Personality Disorder (OCPD):** OCPD is characterized by an obsession with order, perfectionism, and control. While individuals with AvPD may exhibit perfectionistic tendencies, the primary focus of AvPD is social avoidance and fear of criticism, rather than perfectionism.

5. **Schizoid Personality Disorder (SPD):** SPD is distinguished by a lack of interest in social relationships and a preference for solitary activities. Individuals with AvPD may also prefer solitude, but their motivation is different. In AvPD, avoidance of social situations is driven by a fear of rejection, whereas in SPD avoidance is driven by a lack of interest in social interactions.

6. **Avoidant Restrictive Food Intake Disorder (ARFID):** ARFID is characterized by a restrictive diet due to fear of aversive consequences such as choking or vomiting. Individuals with AvPD may also exhibit food-related avoidance behaviors, but these behaviors are

usually driven by a fear of judgment or criticism rather than a fear of physical harm.

7. **Post-traumatic stress disorder (PTSD):** PTSD is distinguished by intrusive memories, avoidance of triggers, negative changes in mood and cognitive patterns, and hyperarousal. While individuals with AvPD may experience trauma-related symptoms, their avoidance is more focused on interpersonal relationships and social events than on specific trauma-related triggers.

8. **Major Depressive (MDD):** MDD is defined by persistent feelings of sadness, hopelessness, and loss of interest in activities. While individuals with AvPD may experience depressive symptoms, the primary focus of the disorder is social avoidance and fear of rejection, not mood disorders.

9. **Borderline personality disorder (BPD):** BPD is distinguished by unstable relationships, impulsive behavior, and intense emotions. While individuals with AvPD may struggle with relationships and emotions, the main characteristic of AvPD is a continuous pattern of social inhibition, feelings of inadequacy, and hypersensitivity to negative judgment, which are not primary features of BPD.

10. **Narcissistic Personality Disorder (NPD):** NPD is distinguished by a grandiose sense of self-importance, a desire for admiration, and a lack of empathy. While individuals with AvPD may struggle with self-esteem and interpersonal interactions, the primary focus of the disorder is social avoidance and fear of rejection, rather than on a grandiose self-image.

11. **Depressive Personality Disorder (DPD):** DPD is distinguished by a pervasive pattern of depressive symptoms, such as sadness, pessimism, and low self-esteem. While individuals with AvPD may suffer depressive symptoms, the main hallmark is social avoidance and fear of rejection, rather than a general sense of sadness or pessimism.

12. **Attention Deficit/Hyperactivity Disorder (ADHD):** ADHD symptoms include inattention, hyperactivity, and impulsivity. While individuals with AvPD may struggle with attention and impulse control, the primary focus of the disorder is social avoidance and fear of rejection, rather than on attention and hyperactivity issues.

13. **Substance Use Disorders:** Individuals with AvPD may be at an increased risk to develop substance use disorders as a symptom-management strategy. However, the primary focus of AvPD is on social avoidance and fear of rejection, rather than on substance use.

14. **Autism Spectrum Disorder (ASD):** ASD is characterized by difficulties with social interaction and communication, as well as restricted and repetitive behaviors. While some ASD symptoms coincide with AvPD, such as social difficulties, AvPD's underlying motivations and behaviors are driven by a fear of rejection and criticism rather than by deficits in social understanding.

15. **Schizotypal Personality Disorder (STPD):** STPD is characterized by eccentric behavior, odd beliefs or magical thinking, and social anxiety. While individuals with AvPD may experience social anxiety, the primary focus of the disorder is on social avoidance and fear of rejection, rather than eccentric behaviors or odd beliefs.

In conclusion, diagnosing AvPD requires careful consideration of differential diagnoses in order to ensure an accurate assessment. Clinicians can provide appropriate treatment and support individuals with AvPD by understanding the differences between it and other conditions. Remember, seeking help from a qualified mental health professional is the first step toward understanding and managing AvPD.

Assessing Severity and Functional Impairment.

Assessing the severity and functional impairment of Avoidant Personality Disorder (AvPD) is critical for developing an effective treatment plan and understanding how the disorder affects a person's life. Listed below are some of the approaches for assessing the severity and functional impairment of AvPD.

1. **Clinical Interview:** A thorough clinical interview with a mental health professional is essential to determine the severity of AvPD symptoms. During the interview, the clinician will inquire about your symptoms', their duration and intensity, as well as how they affect your everyday life.

2. **Self-Report Questionnaires:** Various self-report questionnaires can be used to assess the severity of AvPD symptoms. These questionnaires ask you to rate the frequency and intensity of your symptoms, which is useful information for clinicians.

3. **Structured Clinical Interviews:** The Structured Clinical Interview for DSM-5 (SCID-5) can be used to assess the severity of AvPD symptoms. These interviews

follow a specific format and ask detailed questions about your symptoms to determine if you meet the criteria for AvPD.

4. **Behavioral observation:** Observing your behavior in different social contexts can provide useful information about the severity of your AvPD symptoms. Clinicians may observe your social relationships, body language, and level of discomfort.

5. **Functional Impairment scales:** Functional impairment scales, such as the Global Assessment of Functioning (GAF) scale, can be used to determine how AvPD affects your daily functioning. These scales rate your ability to perform in a various areas, including work, relationships with others, and self-care.

6. **Interviews with Families and Caregivers:** Family members or caregivers can provide valuable information about the effects of AvPD on your life. They can describe how your symptoms affect your relationships, daily activities, and overall health.

7. **Psychological Test:** Psychological tests, such as personality assessments, can assist in assessing the severity of AvPD symptoms. These tests provide additional information about your personality traits and how they may contribute to your symptoms.

8. **Functional Magnetic Resonance Imaging (fMRI):** While not commonly used, fMRI can provide insights into the brain activity related with AvPD. This imaging technique can help researchers better understand the neural mechanisms underlying the disorder and may aid in assessing severity.

9. **Life Events and Difficulties Schedule (LEDS):** The LEDS is a structured interview that evaluates the incidence and impact of life events and challenges. It can assist in determining stressors that may contribute to the severity of AvPD symptoms.

10. **Structured Clinical Assessment of Maladaptive Traits (SCAMT):** SCAMT is a structured interview for assessing maladaptive personality traits, especially those associated with AvPD. It can provide extensive information on the severity of various AvPD-related traits.

11. **Social Functioning Scale (SFS):** SFS is a self-report questionnaire that assesses various aspects of social functioning, including social engagement, communication skills, and interpersonal connections. It can help to determine the effect of AvPD on social functioning.

12. **Work and Social Adjustment Scale (WSAS):** The WSAS is a self-report questionnaire that assesses the impact of mental health problems on various areas of functioning, such as work, social life, and everyday activities. It can help assess the functional impairment caused by AvPD.

13. **Quality of Life Scale (QoLS):** QoLS is a self-report questionnaire that assesses total quality of life, which includes physical health, psychological well-being, social interactions, and the environment. It can help assess the effect of AvPD on overall quality of life.

14. **Clinical Global Impression Scale (CGI):** The CGI is a clinician-rated scale that assesses the overall severity of illness and global improvement. It can provide a broad assessment of the severity of AvPD symptoms and functional impairment.

15. **Structured Assessment of Personality Abbreviated Scale (SAPA-S):** SAPA-S is a self-report questionnaire that assesses maladaptive personality traits, especially those associated with AvPD. It can provide a swift assessment of the severity of AvPD traits.

Assessing the severity and functional impairment of AvPD requires a comprehensive approach that combines various assessment methods. By gathering information from multiple sources, clinicians can develop a holistic understanding of your symptoms and design a treatment strategy to meet your specific needs. Remember, seeking help from a qualified mental health professional is the first step towards better understanding and managing AvPD.

Considering Cultural and Contextual Factors.

When diagnosing and assessing Avoidant Personality Disorder (AvPD), it is critical to take into consideration cultural and environmental factors that can influence how the disorder manifests and is perceived. These factors have a substantial impact on how symptoms are expressed, the level of stigma attached to mental health issues, and the availability of appropriate treatment options. Let's explore some important cultural and contextual considerations in the diagnosis and assessment of AvPD.

1. **Cultural norms and values:** Cultural norms and beliefs can influence how individuals experience and express symptoms of AvPD. For example, in cultures that value collectivism above individualism, social

withdrawal and avoidance may be tolerated or even encouraged. On the other hand, in cultures that value social harmony and conformity, similar symptoms may be stigmatized more.

2. **Language and Communication Style:** Language barriers and communication styles can have an impact on the assessment of AvPD. Some cultures may have specific ways of expressing emotions or social behaviors that differ from Western norms. Clinicians need to be mindful of these differences and adjust their assessment methods accordingly.

3. **Family and Social Support Systems:** The role of family and social support systems can differ widely amongst cultures. In some cultures, family involvement in mental health concerns is expected and can help with treatment. In other cultures, requesting help for mental health problems may be viewed negatively, resulting in delayed diagnosis and treatment.

4. **Stigma & Mental Health Literacy:** Stigma associated with mental health concerns can influence how AvPD is perceived and diagnosed. Individuals in cultures where mental health disorders are strongly stigmatized may be less inclined to seek help or disclose their symptoms. This can result in an underdiagnosis and treatment of AvPD.

5. Cultural Beliefs on Personality and Identity:
Cultural beliefs on personality and identity can influence how AvPD is understood and diagnosed. For example, in cultures that place a high value on personal responsibility and self-reliance, AvPD symptoms may be attributed to character flaws rather than a mental health disorder.

6. Access to Mental Health Services: Access to mental health care might vary widely depending on cultural and contextual factors. Some cultures may have limited access to mental health services or lack culturally competent care. This can lead to delays in diagnosing and treating AvPD.

7. Migration and Acculturation: Acculturation can play a significant role on the expression of AvPD symptoms in individuals who have just moved to a new country. The stress of adapting to a new country and navigating cultural differences might worsen symptoms of AvPD.

8. Spiritual and religious beliefs: Spiritual and religious beliefs can also shape how AvPD is perceived and treated. Spiritual or religious practices may be integrated into mental health treatment in some cultures, while in others, they may be seen as separate or even in conflict with Western approaches to mental health.

In conclusion, cultural and contextual factors must be considered while diagnosing and assessing AvPD. Clinicians must understand how these factors influence symptom presentation, help-seeking behavior, and treatment preferences. By taking a culturally sensitive approach, clinicians can provide more effective and complete care to individuals with AvPD.

Challenges in Diagnosing AvPD.

Diagnosing Avoidant Personality Disorder (AvPD) can be challenging due to a variety of factors that complicate the assessment process. These challenges can stem from the nature of the disorder itself, as well as external factors that impact how symptoms are recognized and interpreted. Let's examine some of the key challenges in diagnosing AvPD.

1. **Overlap with Other Disorders:** AvPD shares symptoms with other personality disorders, including Social Anxiety Disorder (SAD) and Dependent Personality Disorder (DPD). The overlap in symptoms can make it difficult to distinguish between these disorders and accurately diagnose AvPD.

2. **Co-occurring Disorders:** AvPD often co-occurs with other mental health disorders, including depression, anxiety disorders, and substance use disorders. These co-occurring disorders can mask or intensify symptoms of AvPD, making it challenging to identify and diagnose.

3. **Symptom Variability:** The symptoms of AvPD can vary widely from person to person and may also fluctuate over time. This unpredictability can make it difficult to establish a consistent pattern of behavior that is distinct to AvPD.

4. **Subjectivity of Symptoms:** Many of the symptoms of AvPD, such as fear of rejection and avoidance of social situations, are subjective and difficult to measure subjectively. This subjectivity can lead to differences in how clinicians perceive symptoms.

5. **Limited Awareness and Insight:** Individuals with AvPD may have limited awareness or insight into their symptoms, making it difficult for them to adequately recount their experiences during an examination. This lack of awareness may also influence their willingness to seek help and engage in treatment.

6. **Stigma & Shame:** The stigma surrounding mental health disorders, including personality disorders, can lead to feelings of shame and reluctance to seek help.

This stigma can prevent a proper diagnosis and management of AvPD.

7. **Cultural and Contextual Factors:** Cultural norms and values, as well as contextual factors such as socioeconomic status and healthcare access, can influence how AvPD symptoms are expressed and interpreted. When assessing for AvPD, clinicians must be sensitive to these factors.

8. **Complexity of Diagnosis:** Diagnosing AvPD requires a comprehensive evaluation that takes into account the individual's history, symptoms, and functioning in every area of life. This complexity can make it challenging to reach a definitive diagnosis, especially when symptoms are subtle or overlap with other disorders.

In conclusion, diagnosing AvPD can be challenging due to several factors. Clinicians must be aware of these challenges and conduct assessments that are both comprehensive and culturally sensitive. By addressing these challenges, clinicians can improve the accuracy of AvPD diagnoses and provide more effective treatment to individuals with this disorder.

CHAPTER SIX.

Treatment Approaches.

Psychotherapy, also known as talk therapy, is a cornerstone in the treatment of Avoidant Personality Disorder (AvPD). It provides a supportive and understanding environment where you can explore your thoughts, feelings, and behaviors. Here's a list of how psychotherapy can be beneficial in managing AvPD:

1. **Cognitive Behavioral Therapy (CBT):** CBT is one of the most prevalent and effective forms of therapy for AvPD. It focuses on identifying and correcting negative thought patterns and beliefs that contribute to avoidance behavior. Recognizing and modifying these patterns helps you to develop more adaptive ways of thinking and responding to social situations.

2. **Exposure Therapy:** Exposure therapy gradually exposes you to fearful social situations in a controlled and supportive setting. The goal is to help you address and overcome your anxieties, hence diminishing

avoidance behavior over time. This approach can be highly effective in building confidence and reducing anxiety associated with social interactions.

3. **Social Skills Training:** Many individuals with AvPD struggle with social skills such as initiating conversations, maintaining eye contact, and understanding social cues. Social skills training can help you develop these skills by providing instruction, role-playing, and feedback. This can help you gain confidence and comfort in social situations.

4. **Psychodynamic Therapy:** Psychodynamic therapy seeks to uncover unconscious beliefs and emotions that may contribute to AvPD. You can gain a better understanding of your behavior and make positive changes by learning about underlying issues such as past traumas or relationship patterns.

5. **Interpersonal therapy (IPT):** IPT aims to improve interpersonal relationships and communication skills. It assists you in identifying and addressing problematic relationship patterns, establishing social support networks, and developing healthier ways of interacting with others.

6. **Supportive Therapy:** Supportive therapy offers a compassionate and nonjudgmental space where you can share your thoughts while receiving support and encouragement. It can help reduce the feelings of isolation and loneliness often experienced by many individuals with AvPD.

7. **Group therapy:** Group therapy allows you to connect with others who have had similar experiences and struggles. It provides a supportive space for developing social skills, receiving feedback, and building relationships. Group therapy can also help you realize that you are not alone in your struggles.

8. **Mindfulness-Based Therapies:** Mindfulness-based therapies, such as Mindfulness-Based Stress Reduction (MBSR) and Mindfulness-Based Cognitive Therapy (MBCT), can help you become more aware of your thoughts and feelings without passing judgment. This improved self-awareness may assist you in better understanding and managing your AvPD symptoms.

In conclusion, psychotherapy provides a variety of approaches to help you manage and overcome Avoidant Personality Disorder. Working with a qualified therapist can help you gain the confidence and insights needed to navigate social situations and build more fulfilling relationships. Remember that therapy is a collaborative process, and your therapist is there to support you on your journey to recovery.

Medication Options and Considerations.

While psychotherapy is the primary treatment for Avoidant Personality Disorder (AvPD), medication can help manage symptoms, especially if they co-occur with other mental health disorders. Let's explore medication options and considerations for treating AvPD.

1. **Selective Serotonin Reuptake Inhibitors (SSRIs):** SSRIs are commonly prescribed antidepressants that can help alleviate anxiety and depression symptoms, which are common in individuals with AvPD. These medications work by increasing serotonin levels in the brain, thereby improving mood and reducing anxiety.

2. **Serotonin and Norepinephrine Reuptake Inhibitors (SNRIs):** SNRIs are another class of antidepressant that can be used to treat AvPD. SNRIs, like SSRIs, increase serotonin and norepinephrine levels

in the brain, which can enhance mood and reduce anxiety.

3. **Benzodiazepines:** Benzodiazepines are a class of medications that can help alleviate acute anxiety symptoms, such as panic attacks. They are usually prescribed for short-term use due to the risk of tolerance, dependence, and withdrawal symptoms.

4. **Beta Blockers:** Beta-blockers are medications that can help reduce the physical symptoms of anxiety, such as rapid heart rate and trembling. They are often used in situations where anxiety is triggered by specific events, such as public speaking or performance anxiety.

5. **Antidepressants with anxiolytic properties:** Some antidepressants, such as tricyclic antidepressants (TCAs) and mirtazapine, have anxiolytic (anti-anxiety) properties and may be used to treat AvPD, especially when anxiety symptoms are prominent.

6. **Antipsychotic Medication:** In some cases, antipsychotic medications may be administered to manage severe anxiety or paranoid thoughts caused by AvPD. However, these medications are usually reserved for cases where other treatments have proven ineffective.

7. **Stimulants:** Stimulant medications, such as those used to treat attention-deficit/hyperactivity disorder (ADHD), are sometimes used off-label to help improve focus and concentration in individuals with AvPD. However, their use in AvPD is controversial and should be carefully considered.

Considerations and precautions.

When considering medication for AvPD, it is critical to weigh the potential benefits against the risks and side effects. Some medications can cause side effects such as weight gain, sexual dysfunction, or gastrointestinal problems. Additionally, medications should be prescribed and monitored by a qualified healthcare professional to ensure their safety and effectiveness.

In conclusion, while medication can be a helpful adjunct to psychotherapy in the treatment of AvPD, it is not a stand-alone treatment. It is essential to work closely with a healthcare provider to determine the most appropriate treatment plan for your individual needs. Combining medication with psychotherapy and other supportive interventions can effectively help you manage AvPD symptoms and improve your overall quality of life.

Group Therapy and Support Groups.

Group therapy and support groups can be valuable components of treatment for Avoidant Personality Disorder (AvPD). These settings provide a supportive and understanding environment where you can connect with others who share similar experiences and challenges. Here's explore how group therapy and support groups are beneficial in managing AvPD.

1. **Shared Experiences:** One of the most significant advantages of group therapy and support groups is the ability to interact with others who understand what you're going through. Being part of a community of others who face similar struggles can help you feel less alone and more understood.

2. **Social Skills Practice:** Group therapy provides a safe space to practice social skills in a supportive environment. You can try out new ways of engaging with others, receive feedback, and build confidence in social situations.

3. **Feedback and validation:** In a group setting, you can receive feedback and validation from others, which can help you gain insight into your own behavior and beliefs. This is especially helpful for those with AvPD, who may struggle with self-esteem and acceptance.

4. **Learn from others:** Hearing about other group members' experiences and coping strategies can provide you with new perspectives and ideas for managing your AvPD symptoms. You may also learn about about resources and treatment options that you were previously unaware of.

5. **Building Relationships:** Group therapy and support groups can help you form meaningful connections with others who understand and accept you. These relationships can provide you with a sense of belonging and support outside of the group setting.

6. **Normalization of Symptoms:** Being in a group of others with similar symptoms can help to normalize your experiences. This can reduce feelings of shame or embarrassment regarding your symptoms, helping you feel more accepted.

7. **Accountability:** Group therapy can provide a sense of accountability for your progress. Knowing that others are rooting for you and expecting you to show up can motivate you to participate fully in treatment.

8. **Structured Environment:** Group therapy provides a structured environment where you can focus on specific goals and objectives related to your AvPD. The group leader can help guide the discussion and ensure that everyone gets a chance to participate.

Group therapy and support groups can be valuable resources for individuals with Avoidant Personality Disorder. They provide a supportive environment where you can connect with others, practice social skills, and gain insight into your own behavior. By participating in group therapy, you can improve your treatment experience and your overall well-being.

Holistic and Complementary Approaches.

Holistic and complementary approaches can be valuable additions to traditional treatment for Avoidant

Personality Disorder (AvPD). These approaches address the whole person—mind, body, and spirit—and can help improve overall well-being and quality of life. Let's examine some holistic and complementary approaches that could be beneficial for managing AvPD.

1. **Mindfulness and meditation:** Mindfulness practices such as meditation and yoga can help you become more aware of your thoughts, emotions, and physical sensations. These activities can induce relaxation, reduce anxiety, and improve self-awareness, which can be particularly beneficial for individuals who have AvPD.

2. **Exercise and Physical Activity:** Regular exercise can improve both physical and mental health. Exercise causes the release of endorphins, which are natural mood lifters that can help reduce symptoms of anxiety and depression. Engaging in physical activity can help also help boost self-esteem and improve body image, which are significant concerns for individuals with AvPD.

3. **Nutrition and Diet:** A nutritious diet can support general health and well-being. Certain foods, such as those abundant in omega-3 fatty acids, antioxidants, and vitamins, may have a specific impact on mental health. Eating regular, nutritious meals can also help in stabilizing mood and energy levels.

4. **Herbal Remedies and Supplements:** Some individuals find that using herbal medicines and supplements relieves their anxiety and depression symptoms. Herbs like St. John's Wort and passionflower, for example, are sometimes used to help with anxiety and mood improvement. However, before starting any new supplement regimen, consult with your healthcare provider.

5. **Acupuncture and acupressure:** Traditional Chinese medicine practices, such as acupuncture and acupressure, can help to balance the body's energy and promote relaxation. Some people find these practices to be helpful in reducing anxiety and stress.

6. **Arts and Music Therapy:** Creative therapies, such as art and music therapy, can provide a creative outlet for expressing emotions and reducing stress. These therapies can be particularly beneficial for individuals who have trouble expressing themselves verbally.

7. **Aromatherapy:** Aromatherapy is the use of essential oils to relax and improve mood. Certain scents, such as lavender and chamomile, are known to have relaxing effects and may help reduce anxiety symptoms.

8. **Holistic Therapy:** Massage therapy, Reiki, and biofeedback are some more holistic therapies that can help you relax and reduce stress. These therapies

aim to balance the body's energy and promote overall well-being.

In conclusion, holistic and complementary approaches can be effective tools for managing AvPD. By incorporating these strategies into your treatment plan, you can improve your general well-being and ability to cope with the challenges of AvPD. It is critical to consult with a healthcare provider to identify which approaches are best for you and to ensure that they complement your existing treatment plan.

CHAPTER SEVEN.

Cognitive Restructuring Techniques.

Cognitive restructuring is a therapeutic technique used in cognitive-behavioral therapy (CBT) to help individuals in identifying and challenging negative or distorted thought patterns. The aim is to replace unhelpful or irrational thoughts with more realistic and balanced ones.

Cognitive Restructuring in Real-life Situations.

How can cognitive restructuring be applied in real-life situations?

Here is an example of how cognitive restructuring can be applied in a real-life situation:

Situation: Lilian has been invited to a social function with her colleagues. However, she is feeling anxious and is considering backing out because she thinks

she would embarrass herself and that no one will like her.

1. **Recognize negative thoughts:** Lilian recognizes her negative thoughts: "I will embarrass myself" and "Nobody will like me."

2. **Evaluate the evidence:** Lilian evaluates the evidence that supports her beliefs. She understands she has previously attended social functions without major humiliation. She also recalls occasions when she received encouraging feedback from colleagues.

3. **Challenge cognitive distortions:** Lilian recognizes cognitive distortions in her own ideas, such as catastrophizing and mind-reading. She admits that she is anticipating the worst without considering alternative possibilities.

4. **Generate alternative thoughts:** Lilian develops alternate, more balanced thoughts, such as "I might feel a little nervous, but that's normal in social situations" and "My colleagues have enjoyed spending time with me."

5. **Reappraise the situation:** Lilian reevaluates the situation, recognizing that her negative thoughts may not accurately reflect reality. She recognizes that social

gatherings can be opportunities to connect with coworkers and engage in enjoyable conversations.

6. **Practice and reinforce new thoughts:** Lilian repeats her alternative thoughts to herself and visualizes herself attending the social gathering calmly and confidently. She reminds herself of the positive experiences she has had in similar situations.

7. **Monitor and challenge ongoing negative thoughts:** During the social gathering, Lilian actively challenges any self-critical or negative thoughts that arise through the cognitive restructuring process. She reminds herself of the alternative thoughts and concentrates on being present in the moment rather than becoming preoccupied with anxious thoughts.

By applying cognitive restructuring techniques, Lilian might progressively transform her mindset from one dominated by negative thinking to one more balanced and realistic. This can help her to manage her anxiety, attend the social gathering, and possibly have a positive social experience.

How long does it usually take for someone's mindset to see a shift in their mindset through cognitive restructuring?

The timeframe for experiencing a shift in mindset through cognitive restructuring varies significantly from person to person. It is determined by various factors, including the individual's commitment to the process, the severity of their cognitive distortions, and the frequency and consistency with which they practice.

Individuals may experience noticeable changes in their thinking patterns relatively quickly in certain situations, whilst others may require more time and effort. Cognitive restructuring is a skill that requires practice and repetition to become more natural and automatic.

For some people, a few weeks or months of consistent practice may be sufficient to start noticing positive changes in their thinking and emotional responses. However, for others, it may take several months, or even longer to see significant shifts in their mindset.

It is essential to approach cognitive restructuring with patience and realistic expectations. It is not a quick-fix solution, but rather a gradual process of rewiring ingrained patterns of thinking. Progress can be nonlinear, with ups and downs along the way.

Working with a mental health professional, such as a therapist or psychologist, can be beneficial in guiding the cognitive restructuring process while also providing support and feedback. They can help tailor the approach to specific needs and monitor progress over time.

Remember that the purpose of cognitive restructuring isn't to eliminate all negative thoughts or achieve perfection in thinking. Rather, it aims to develop more balanced, realistic, and adaptable thought patterns, which can contribute to improved emotional well-being and more effective coping strategies.

What coping strategies can be developed through cognitive restructuring?

Cognitive restructuring can help individuals develop various kinds of coping strategies that promote more adaptive and resilient responses to challenging situations. Here are a few examples:

1. **Thought stopping:** When individuals notice a negative or distorted thought coming up, they can practice thought stopping. This involves mentally saying "stop" or picturing a red stop sign to interrupt the thought and keep it from escalating further.

2. **Reframing:** Reframing is the conscious shift in one's perspective on a situation to see it in a more positive or balanced light. This can involve finding alternative explanations, focusing on the bright side, or considering the potential for personal growth or learning.

3. **Self-compassion:** Cognitive restructuring can help individuals develop self-compassion by challenging self-critical thoughts and replacing them with kinder, more understanding self-talk. This can involve treating oneself with the same care and compassion as one would give to a friend in a similar situation.

4. **Positive affirmations:** Affirmations are positive statements that individuals tell themselves to combat negative self-talk. Cognitive restructuring allows individuals to identify and create affirmations that challenge negative thoughts while reinforcing more positive and empowering thoughts.

5. **Cognitive rehearsal:** Cognitive restructuring allows individuals to mentally rehearse challenging situations and practice responding in more adaptive and effective ways. Individuals can boost their confidence and problem-solving skills by imagining and picturing successful outcomes.

6. **Mindfulness:** Cognitive restructuring can be combined with mindfulness techniques to cultivate present-moment awareness and nonjudgmental observation of thoughts and emotions. Mindfulness can help individuals separate their thoughts from their emotional reactions, allowing for more intentional and balanced responses.

7. **Problem-solving:** Cognitive restructuring can improve problem-solving abilities by encouraging individuals to challenge negative assumptions or limitations and consider alternative solutions. It promotes a flexible and constructive approach to overcoming challenges and finding effective solutions.

8. **Gratitude practice:** Cognitive restructuring can help individuals develop the habit of focusing on and appreciating the positive aspects of their lives. Practicing gratitude, such as keeping a gratitude journal or expressing appreciation to others, can help you change your focus away from negative thoughts and into a more positive mindset.

These coping strategies, when combined with cognitive restructuring techniques, can help individuals manage stress, regulate their emotions, and approach difficult situations with greater resilience and adaptability. It's crucial to remember that different strategies may work better for different people, so it can be helpful to experiment and try different techniques to see what works best for you.

CHAPTER EIGHT.

Strategies for Self-management and Coping.

Building Self-awareness and Insight.

Self-awareness and insight are crucial components for managing Avoidant Personality Disorder (AvPD). Developing a better understanding of yourself, your thoughts, emotions, and behaviors can help you identify and challenge negative patterns while also developing healthy coping mechanisms. Let's look at some strategies for building self-awareness and insight in the context of AvPD.

1. **Mindfulness Practice:** Mindfulness is the practice of paying attention to the present moment without judgment. Mindfulness can help you become more aware of your thoughts, emotions, and bodily sensations, helping you to identify patterns and triggers that contribute to avoidant behavior.

2. **Journaling:** Keeping a journal allows you to document your thoughts, feelings, and behaviors throughout time. This can provide useful insights into your patterns and help you in identifying situations or triggers that lead to avoidance. Writing can also be a therapeutic technique to vent emotions and gain clarity.

3. **Therapy:** Therapy, particularly modalities such as psychodynamic therapy or cognitive-behavioral therapy (CBT), can assist you in understanding your thoughts and behaviors. A therapist can help you with recognizing underlying issues and developing strategies for challenging negative beliefs and behaviors.

4. **Self-Reflection:** Reflecting on your experiences and reactions can help you become more self-aware. Consider journaling prompts like "What triggered my avoidance today?" or "How did I respond to a challenging social situation?"

5. **Seeking feedback:** Asking trusted friends, family members, or a therapist for feedback can help you with a new perspective on your behavior. This can help you uncover blind spots and areas for growth.

6. **Self-Compassion:** Self-compassion can be practiced by being kind and understanding to yourself. Avoid self-criticism and negative self-talk, as they can hinder self-awareness and insight.

7. **Identifying Core Beliefs:** Investigate the basic assumptions that drive your avoidance behavior. These beliefs are often negative and self-limiting, such as "I'm not good enough" or "I'll be rejected if I'm myself." Recognizing and challenging these beliefs can help you gain more balanced opinions regarding yourself and others.

8. **Behavioral Experiments:** Conduct behavioral experiments to test your beliefs and assumptions. For example, if you believe that others will judge you harshly, deliberately put yourself in a social scenario and observe how others actually react.

9. **Emotional Regulation:** Learn how to recognize and regulate your emotions. Deep breathing, gradual muscular relaxation, and mindfulness meditation are all strategies that can help you stay calm and focused in tough situations.

10. **Setting Realistic Goals:** Set tiny, attainable goals for yourself to gradually tackle the situations that trigger your avoidance. Celebrate your accomplishments, no matter no matter how small, to boost confidence and motivation.

In conclusion, building self-awareness and insight is a continuous process that can substantially help individuals with AvPD. Mindfulness, journaling, therapy, and self-reflection can help you develop a deeper understanding of yourself and your avoidant behavior. This increased awareness can assist you in challenging negative patterns and developing effective coping strategies, ultimately leading to a more rewarding life.

Challenging Negative Thoughts and Beliefs.

Negative thoughts and beliefs are common in individuals with Avoidant Personality Disorder (AvPD). These thoughts can exacerbate feelings of inadequacy, fear of rejection, and avoidance of social situations. However, learning to challenge and reframe these negative thoughts is essential for managing AvPD. Let's explore a few strategies for challenging negative thoughts and beliefs.

1. **Identifying Negative Thoughts:** The first step towards challenging negative thoughts is to become aware of them. Pay attention to your inner dialogue and observe when you're engaging self-critical or self-defeating thoughts.

2. **Questioning Evidence:** When you notice a negative thought, ask yourself for evidence to back it up. Are there any facts or experiences that contradict this thought? For example, if you think "I'll never fit in," push yourself by recalling moments when you felt accepted or included.

3. **Consider Alternative Explanations:** Instead of jumping to negative conclusions, explore other possibilities for a situation. For example, if someone does not respond to your message, it is not necessarily because they dislike you; they could simply be busy or distracted.

4. **Reframing Negative Thoughts:** Once you've identified a negative thought, consider reframing it in a more positive or balanced manner. For example, instead of thinking, "I'm a failure," you could say, "I've had setbacks, but I'm learning and growing."

5. **Practicing Self-Compassion:** Treat yourself with the same love and understanding that you would extend to a friend. Acknowledge that it's alright to make mistakes and that nobody is perfect.

6. **Cognitive restructuring:** This strategy requires actively challenging and correcting negative thought patterns. Replace your negative thoughts with more realistic and pleasant ones. For example, if you

think "no one likes me," challenge this by considering people who appreciate you.

7. **Using Affirmations:** Positive affirmations can help you counteract negative self-talk. To reinforce positive thoughts about yourself, repeat affirmations such as "I deserve to be happy," "I am lovable," or "I am worthy."

8. **Mindful Practice:** Mindfulness allows you to observe your thoughts without judgment. By practicing mindfulness, you can learn to recognize negative thoughts as fleeting events rather than absolute truths.

9. **Seeking Support:** Share your negative thoughts with a trusted friend, family member, or therapist. Talking about your thoughts can provide a new perspective and allow you to challenge them more effectively.

10. **Behavioral Experiments:** Test the validity of your negative beliefs through behavioral experiments. For example, if you believe that speaking up in a group will result in criticism, try it and observe the actual responses.

In conclusion, challenging negative thoughts and beliefs is a crucial aspect of managing AvPD. You can change how you perceive yourself and the world around you by becoming more aware of your thoughts, questioning their validity, and reframing them in a more positive light. Remember that changing negative thought patterns requires time and effort, so be patient and compassionate with yourself as you work towards more positive self-perceptions.

Gradual Exposure and Behavioral Experiments.

Gradual exposure and behavioral experiments are two effective methods for managing Avoidant Personality Disorder (AvPD). These strategies involve gradually facing scary situations and testing negative beliefs, which helps you build confidence and reduce avoidance. Let's examine how using these strategies can help you manage AvPD.

1. **Understanding Gradual Exposure:** Gradual exposure involves facing terrifying situations in stages, starting with less intimidating situations and then progressing to challenging ones. This approach allows you to gradually build your confidence and tolerance for anxiety.

2. Identifying Avoidable Situations: Begin by identifying situations or activities that you tend to avoid due to fear or discomfort. These may include social events, work-related tasks, or personal activities that trigger anxiety or feelings of inadequacy.

3. Create a Hierarchy: Once you've identified the circumstances to avoid, create a hierarchy of these situations from least to most anxiety-provoking. For example, if you're afraid of public speaking, your hierarchy could contain activities such as speaking to a small group of friends, then to a bigger group, and finally to an formal audience.

4. Starting Small: Start with the least daunting issue in your hierarchy. Gradually expose yourself to this situation, allowing yourself to experience the anxiety while also noticing how it fades over time.

5. Using Relaxation Techniques: Deep breathing, progressive muscle relaxation, or mindfulness can help you manage anxiety as you confront feared situations. These approaches can help you remain calm and focused.

6. Tracking Progress: Keep track of your progress as you move through the hierarchy. Take note of any improvements in your feelings of fear or avoidance, and celebrate your accomplishments, no matter how insignificant.

7. **Confronting Negative Beliefs:** Pay attention to any negative beliefs or thoughts that arise when you expose yourself to terrifying situations. Challenge these beliefs by conducting behavioral experiments to test their validity.

8. **Reflecting on Experiences:** After each exposure or experiment, take some time to reflect on your experience. Take note of any changes in your thoughts, feelings and behaviors, and analyze how these experiences challenge your negative beliefs.

9. **Seeking Support:** Gradual exposure and behavioral experiments might be difficult, so seek assistance from a therapist, support group, or someone you can trust. They can provide encouragement and guidance as you work through your fears.

In conclusion, gradual exposure and behavioral experiments are effective strategies for managing AvPD. By gradually confronting terrifying situations and testing negative beliefs, you can build confidence, reduce avoidance, and develop healthier coping mechanisms. Remember that progress requires time and patience, so be gentle with yourself as you embark on this journey of self-discovery and growth.

Developing Healthy Relationships and Boundaries.

Individuals with Avoidant Personality Disorder (AvPD) must prioritize the establishment of healthy relationships and boundaries. It involves understanding your own needs, setting boundaries, and building trust in your relationships. Here's a detailed guide on how to navigate these aspects:

1. **Understanding Your Needs:** In healthy relationships, you must understand and communicate your needs. Start by identifying what you need in a relationship, such as emotional support, understanding, or space. Recognize that it is normal to have needs and that expressing them is essential for building healthy relationships.

2. **Setting Boundaries:** Boundaries are essential for safeguarding your emotional health. They determine what is acceptable and unacceptable in your relationships. Setting boundaries might be difficult for people with AvPD, but it's an important step toward building good relationships. Identify your limits and

communicate them clearly and assertively. For example, if you need alone time, tell your partner or friends without feeling guilty.

3. **Building Trust:** Trust is the foundation of all healthy relationships. It involves believing in the reliability, truthfulness, and ability of others. Building trust takes time and effort. Start by trusting yourself and gradually opening up to others. Understand that not everyone will hurt you, and it is okay to let people in.

4. **Effective Communication:** Communication is essential for creating successful relationships. Practice being open, honest, and assertive in communication. Express your thoughts, feelings and needs clearly while actively listening to others. Avoidance can be a coping mechanism for AvPD, but learning to communicate effectively will help you build stronger connections.

5. **Identifying unhealthy patterns:** It is important to identify and address unhealthy patterns in your relationships. This could involve people-pleasing, avoiding conflict, or seeking validation from others. Be mindful of these patterns and work towards changing them. Therapy can help you understand and modify these behaviors.

6. **Seeking Help:** Building healthy relationships and setting boundaries can be challenging, particularly for

individuals with AvPD. Consider seeking the assistance of a therapist or becoming a member of a support group. Therapy can provide you with tools and strategies for effectively navigating relationships.

7. **Self-Care:** Self-care is essential for maintaining healthy relationships. Look after your physical, emotional, and mental wellbeing. Engage in activities that will make you joyful and relaxed. Remember that taking care of yourself allows you to be present and available in your relationships.

In conclusion, developing healthy relationships and boundaries is an ongoing process requiring self-awareness, communication, and care. Understanding your needs, setting boundaries, and building trust can help you cultivate meaningful connections that support your well-being.

CHAPTER NINE.

Living With Avoidant Personality Disorder.

Living with Avoidant Personality Disorder (AvPD) can have significant impact in many areas of your life, including relationships, work, and daily activities. The fear of rejection, criticism, and embarrassment associated with AvPD can make it difficult to actively engage in these areas. Let's look at how AvPD affects your relationships, career, and daily life, as well as strategies for handling these issues.

Impact on Relationships.

AvPD can greatly affect your relationships, making it difficult to establish and maintain deep connections with others. You may avoid social interactions, be afraid of intimacy, or feel inadequate in social situations. This can contribute to feelings of loneliness, isolation, and low self-esteem.

Strategies for Managing Relationship Challenges:

- **Seek Support:** Consider therapy or support groups to learn coping strategies and build social skills.

- **Practice Assertiveness:** Learn how to express your needs and boundaries in relationships.

- **Challenge Negative Beliefs:** Work on changing your negative beliefs about yourself and others.

- **Build Trust Gradually:** Start by taking small steps to build trust in your relationships.

Impact on Work.

AvPD can interfere with your work life by causing difficulties in social interactions, fear of criticism, and avoidance of situations that require teamwork or public speaking. This might lead to problems at work, such as difficulty advancing in your career or maintaining employment.

Strategies for Managing Work Challenges.

- **Communication Skills:** Practice effective communication and assertiveness in the workplace.

- **Set Realistic Goals:** To prevent feelings of overwhelm, break down tasks into smaller, manageable steps.

- **Seek Feedback:** Ask for feedback from colleagues to gain a more objective perspective.

- **Professional Support:** Consider career counseling or coaching to explore career options and strategies for success.

Impact on Daily Life.

AvPD can disrupt your daily life by making you avoid social activities, work-related events, and even routine tasks that involve interaction with others. This can cause feelings of loneliness, isolation, and a sense of missing out on life's experiences.

Strategies for Managing Daily Life Challenges.

- **Routine and Structure:** Sticking to a regular schedule might help you feel more stable and predictable.

- **Self-Care:** Self-care entails giving precedence to activities that foster relaxation and overall wellness.

-**Challenge Avoidance Behaviors:** Gradually expose yourself to frightening situations in order to build confidence.

-**Mindfulness Practice:** Practice mindfulness to stay in the moment and reduce anxiety about the future.

In conclusion, living with AvPD can pose particular challenges in relationships, work, and daily life. However, by understanding these challenges and implementing strategies to manage them, you may improve your quality of life and well-being. Remember that seeking help from a mental health professional is an important step in managing AvPD and improving your overall mental health.

Impact on Academic Challenges.

Living with Avoidant Personality Disorder (AvPD) can have a major impact on academic performance and overall academic experience. The fear of criticism, rejection, and failure that characterizes AvPD can impede learning and achievement. Let's examine how AvPD affects academic issues and how to manage them effectively.

1. **Social Interactions:** AvPD can make it challenging to participate in classroom discussions, work on group assignments, or seek help from teachers. You may avoid these situations out of fear of being criticized or embarrassed.

2. **Fear of Failure:** Individuals with AvPD frequently experience a significant fear of failure, which can contribute to procrastination, perfectionism, and avoidance of challenging tasks. This fear can hinder academic progress and lead to underachievement.

3. **Low Self-esteem:** AvPD can contribute to low self-esteem, making it difficult to believe in your own abilities and academic potential. This can impact motivation and willingness to take academic risks.

4. **Avoiding Academic Settings:** Individuals with AvPD may avoid attending classes, completing assignments, or participating in extracurricular activities for fear of being evaluated negatively. This avoidance might lead to academic failures and missed opportunities for learning and development.

Strategies for Managing Academic Challenges.

1. Seek Help: Reach out to teachers, counselors, or academic advisors for assistance and guidance. They can help you in developing strategies for managing your challenges and, if necessary, provide accommodations.

2. Set Realistic Goals: Divide academic tasks into smaller, more manageable goals. Celebrating your achievements, no matter how small they are, will increase your confidence and motivation.

3. Challenge Negative Thoughts: Practice challenging negative thoughts and beliefs about your academic ability. Change them to more practical and positive ones.

4. Develop Study Skills: Improving your study skills and time management techniques will help you to improve your academic performance. Consider getting help from academic support agencies or tutoring programs.

5. Gradual Exposure: Gradually expose yourself to feared academic situation, such as speaking up in class or requesting assistance from teachers. This can help you gain confidence and reduce avoidance behavior.

6. **Focus on Effort:** Shift your focus from the outcome to the effort you put into your academic studies. Acknowledge your hard work and progress, regardless of the final grade or outcome.

7. **Practice Self-Compassion:** Be kind and understanding to yourself.

Understand that mistakes are inevitable for everyone and that experiencing failure is a normal part of learning.

In conclusion, living with AvPD may present specific difficulties in academic settings. Understanding these challenges and developing techniques to manage them will help you improve your academic performance and general well-being. Remember, seeking support from teachers, counselors, and mental health specialists is an important step toward managing AvPD and academic success.

Challenges and Misconceptions.

Living with Avoidant Personality Disorder (AvPD) can bring a number of difficulties and misconceptions that influence how you perceive yourself and interact with others. Let's examine some of these challenges and misconceptions, as well as how to navigate them.

Challenges:

1. **Difficulty forming relationships:** One of the main challenges of AvPD is the difficulty in establishing and maintaining relationships. Fear of rejection and criticism can make it difficult to trust others and open up emotionally.

2. **Fear of Social Situations:** People with AvPD often experience severe anxiety in social situations, which leads to avoidance of social events, making new friends, or participating in activities that require interaction with others.

3. **Low self-esteem:** Individuals with AvPD often have low self-esteem and a negative self-image. They may feel inadequate or inferior to others, affecting their confidence and self-esteem.

4. **Avoidance of Risk:** Due to their fear of failure and rejection, individuals with AvPD may avoid taking risks or attempting new activities. This can limit personal and professional growth opportunities.

5. **Isolation:** The fear of rejection and criticism can result in social isolation. Individuals with AvPD may avoid social gatherings and prefer to be alone, which can lead to feelings of loneliness and depression.

Misconceptions.

1. **It is Just Shyness:** AvPD is often mistaken for shyness or introversion. Shyness is a normal personality trait, but AvPD is a more severe and debilitating condition that affects daily functioning and relationships.

2. **It is a Choice:** Some people assume that people with AvPD can just "snap out of it" or change their behavior if they choose to. However, AvPD is a complicated mental health condition that requires professional treatment and support.

3. **It is all in your head:** AvPD is sometimes misinterpreted as purely psychological in nature. However, it has biological and genetic components, indicating that it is a legitimate mental health condition requiring medical attention.

4. **You Cannot Get Better:** Another common misconception is that AvPD is a lifelong condition with no chance of improvement. In reality, with the right

treatment and support, individuals with AvPD can learn how to manage their symptoms and live productive lives.

5. It is Just Extreme Introversion: While individuals with AvPD may exhibit introverted traits, the disorder is not simply a more severe form of introversion. AvPD is characterized by a strong fear of rejection and criticism that has a major influence on daily functioning and relationships, going beyond what is usual of introverted individuals.

6. It is Just Social Anxiety: While social anxiety disorder (SAD) and AvPD have certain similarities, they are different conditions. SAD is characterized by fear and anxiety in social situations, whereas AvPD covers a broader fear of rejection, criticism, and inadequacy that extends beyond social interactions to other parts of life.

7. It is Just a Personality Flaw: AvPD is neither a personality flaw nor a sign of weakness. It is a recognized mental health disorder that can have a substantial impact on one's life and well-being. Viewing AvPD as a flaw overlooks the complex interplay of biological, genetic, and environmental factors that contribute to its development.

8. It is untreatable: While AvPD might be difficult to treat, it is not untreatable. Individuals with AvPD can benefit significantly from the right approach, which includes therapy, medication, and support. It is critical to get assistance from mental health experts who specialize in treating personality disorders.

By dispelling these misconceptions and raising awareness and understanding of AvPD, we may foster better empathy and support for those living with this challenging disorder.

CHAPTER TEN.

Overcoming Avoidant Personality Disorder.

Setting realistic goals and expectations.

Setting realistic goals and expectations is an important step towards overcoming avoidant personality disorder (AvPD). It involves identifying attainable goals and understanding how much progress you can realistically made. This process requires self-awareness, patience, and a willingness to push oneself. In this section, we'll examine why having realistic goals is important, how to set them, and how to manage your expectations along the way.

Why Setting Realistic Goals Matter.

Setting realistic goals is essential because it allows you to break down challenging tasks into manageable steps. It enables you to focus on making progress, no matter how small, which boosts confidence and motivation.

Unrealistic goals, on the other hand, can lead to frustration and feelings of failure, reinforcing avoidant behaviors.

How to Set Realistic Goals.

1. **Identify Your Values:** Start by identifying what actually matters to you. Your goals should be consistent with your values in order to provide you with a sense of purpose and motivation.

2. **Break It Down:** Break down large goals into smaller, more doable tasks. This makes them less intimidating and easier to deal with.

3. **Be Specific:** Define your goals clearly. Do not say, "I want to become more social." Instead, say, "This month, I'll attend one social event."

4. **Set Achievable Deadlines:** Give yourself adequate time to complete each step. Rushing may result in mistakes and increased anxiety.

5. **Track Your Progress:** Keep track of your achievements, no matter how small. This can boost your confidence and motivation.

6. **Adjust as Needed:** Be flexible with your goals. If you find that a goal is either too challenging or not difficult enough, adjust it accordingly.

7. **Celebrate Your Success:** Acknowledge and celebrate your achievements. This can help to strengthen positive behaviors.

Managing expectations.

Setting realistic goals is important, but so is managing your expectations. Recovery from AvPD is a journey, and it may not always be linear. Here are some tips for managing your expectations:

1. **Be Patient:** Recovery takes time. Do not expect immediate results. Instead, focus on your progress, no matter how tiny.

2. **Accept Setbacks:** Setbacks are a normal part of any rehabilitation process. Rather than seeing them as failures, consider them opportunities to learn and grow.

3. **Seek Support:** Surround yourself with individuals who will encourage and guide you when needed.

4. **Practice Self-Compassion:** Be kind to yourself. Keep in mind that recovering from AvPD is a challenging process, and it's okay to have bad days.

5. **Focus on the Process, Not Just the Results**: While it is necessary to set goals, it is as critical to focus on your progress. Enjoy the journey, not just the destination.

In conclusion, setting realistic goals and managing your expectations are critical steps toward overcoming avoidant personality disorder. By breaking down your goals, staying flexible, and being patient with yourself, you can make significant progress toward a better, more fulfilling lifestyle.

Creating a supportive environment.

Creating a supportive environment is critical to overcoming avoidant personality disorder (AvPD). It involves surrounding yourself with people who understand your challenges, cultivating healthy relationships, and establishing a network of support. In this part, we'll examine why a supportive environment is essential, how to create one, and what benefits it can bring to your recovery journey.

Why a Supportive Environment Matters.

A supportive environment gives you the encouragement and understanding you need to face the challenges of AvPD. It can make you feel less alone and more connected to others, which is crucial for improving your mental health and well-being. A supportive environment may additionally provide practical help, such as help with everyday tasks or transportation to appointments.

How to Create a Supportive Environment.

1. **Identify Supportive People:** Surround yourself with people who are understanding, compassionate, and nonjudgmental. This could be friends, family members, or support groups.

2. **Communicate Your Needs:** Be open and honest about your struggles and what you expect from others. This can help them provide you the support you need.

3. **Set Boundaries:** While it is necessary to seek help, it is equally important to set boundaries to protect your mental health. Be clear what you can and cannot handle.

4. **Join a Support Group:** Consider joining a support group for others with AvPD. This can provide you with a sense of community and understanding.

5. **Seek Professional Help:** A therapist or counselor can provide you the help and support you need to overcome AvPD. They can also help you develop coping strategies and improve your social skills.

6. **Practice Self-care:** Taking care of oneself is important for maintaining a supportive environment. This involves getting enough rest, eating nutritious foods, and engaging in fun activities.

7. **Stay connected:** Even if you're feeling avoidant, strive to maintain contact with others. This might be as basic as texting someone or briefly attending a social gathering.

Benefits of a Supportive Environment.

1. **Increased Motivation:** When you are surrounded by supportive people, you are more likely to feel motivated to work on overcoming AvPD.

2. **Improved Mental Health:** A supportive environment helps reduce feelings of loneliness and isolation that are common among individuals with AvPD.

3. **Increased self-esteem:** Feeling supported and understood can increase your self-esteem and

confidence, making it easier to confront avoidant behaviors.

4. **Better Coping Skills:** Supportive people can provide you with practical guidance and coping skills for managing AvPD symptoms.

5. **Reduced Stress:** Knowing you have a support network can help reduce stress and anxiety, allowing you to focus on your recovery.

In conclusion, creating a supportive environment is essential for overcoming avoidant personality disorder. By setting boundaries, surrounding yourself with compassionate and understanding people, and seeking professional assistance when needed, you can build a strong support network that will help you on your journey to recovery.

Persistence and Patience in Recovery.

It takes time and perseverance to overcome avoidant personality disorder (AvPD).

Recovery from AvPD is a process that involves confronting your fears, challenging your ideas, and coming up with new ways of thinking and doing. In this section, we'll examine why persistence and patience are important, how to cultivate them, and how they might help you recover.

Why Persistence and Patience Matter.

Persistence is defined as the ability to keep going in the face of adversity. It's about sticking to your goals and refusing to give up, even when things get tough. Patience, on the other hand, refers to the ability to accept delays or difficulties without becoming frustrated or anxious. Both qualities are essential in overcoming AvPD because recovery is often a gradual challenging process.

How to cultivate Persistence and Patience:

1. **Set Realistic Expectations:** Understand that recovering from AvPD requires time and effort. Do not expect immediate results, and be prepared for setbacks along the way.

2. **Focus on Progress, not Perfection:** Instead of striving for perfection, focus on making small, gradual improvements. Celebrate even your small wins.

3. **Practice self-compassion:** Be gentle with yourself. Acknowledge that overcoming AvPD is challenging, and it is normal to struggle at times.

4. **Develop a Growth Mindset:** Rather than seeing setbacks as insurmountable obstacles, consider them opportunities for growth and learning.

5. **Seek Support:** Surround yourself with positive people who will inspire you and keep you motivated.

6. **Break tasks into Manageable Steps:** Rather than attempting to tackle everything at once, divide your goals into smaller, more achievable tasks.

7. **Stay Flexible:** Be willing to adjust your goals and strategies as needed. What works for one person may not work for another, so be willing to try new approaches.

Benefits of Persistence and Patience.

1. **Greater Resilience:** Being persistent and patient can help you become more resilient in the face of challenges.

2. **Improved Mental Health:** Developing these qualities can help reduce stress and anxiety, which are both significant symptoms of AvPD.

3. **Enhanced Problem-Solving Skills:** Persistence and patience can help you improve your problem-solving abilities, allowing you to overcome obstacles more effectively.

4. **Deepened Connections:** Your relationships may improve as a result of your increased ability to connect and interact with others as you grow more persistent and patient.

5. **Increased Self-Confidence:** Overcoming challenges through persistence can enhance your self-confidence and self-esteem.

In conclusion, persistence and patience are important qualities to cultivate in your journey to overcome avoidant personality disorder. Setting realistic expectations, focusing on progress, and getting help when needed will help you develop the resilience and determination needed for lasting recovery.

Celebrating Success and Learning from Setbacks.

Celebrating successes and learning from setbacks are key aspects of growth and progress in the journey to overcome avoidant personality disorder (AvPD). These moments provide opportunities to acknowledge your achievements, no matter how insignificant, and to gain valuable insights from difficulties you may encounter. In this section, we'll have a look at why it's important to celebrate achievements, how to do it effectively, and how to use setbacks as learning opportunities.

Why Celebrating Success Matters.

Celebrating your achievements, no matter how little they may seem, is essential for maintaining motivation and self-esteem. It reinforces positive actions and keeps you focused on your goals.
Furthermore, celebrating successes can improve your mood and overall sense of well-being, making the road to recovery more enjoyable.

How to Celebrate Success.

1. **Acknowledge Your Achievements:** Take the time to recognize and celebrate your accomplishments, no matter how tiny they may appear. This could be completing a task you've been avoiding or participating in a social activity that was difficult for you.

2. **Reward Yourself:** Give yourself something special as a reward for your accomplishments. This could be a simple treat, such as a favorite dessert or a relaxing bath, or a more substantial reward, such as a weekend getaway or a new book.

3. **Share Your Successes:** Share your achievements with those who encourage you. This could be friends, family, or members of a support group. Their positive feedback will help you build on your success and stay motivated.

4. **Reflect on your progress:** Spend some time reflecting on how far you've come. Make a list of your achievements and progress, and refer back to it when you need a motivation boost.

Learn from Setbacks.

Setbacks are a natural part of any journey, including the recovery from AvPD. Instead of viewing setbacks as failures, consider them chances to learn and improve. Here's how you can deal with setbacks in a positive and constructive way:

1. **Identify the Cause:** Try to understand why the setback occurred. Was it due to a specific trigger or situation? Understanding the cause will help you devise measures to avoid similar setbacks in the future.

2. **Focus on Solutions:** Rather than dwelling on the setback, concentrate on finding solutions. Brainstorm ways to overcome the obstacle and get back on track with your goals.

3. **Reach out for Support:** When faced with a setback, do not be afraid to seek help. Talking about your challenges with friends, family, or a therapist might help you gain perspective and find solutions.

4. **Adjust Your Goals:** If necessary, adjust your goals to make them more attainable or achievable. It's okay to reassess and modify your goals as you progress on your journey to recovery.

5. **Practice self-compassion:** Be kind to yourself during setback. Always keep in mind that recovery is a process,

and that setbacks are an inevitable part of that process. Treat yourself with the same compassion you would offer to a friend facing a similar challenge.

In conclusion, celebrating successes and learning from setbacks are essential aspects of overcoming avoidant personality disorder. You can stay motivated and resilient on your recovery journey by acknowledging your achievements, rewarding yourself, and approaching setbacks with a positive mindset.

CHAPTER ELEVEN.

Supporting Someone with AvPD.
Understanding and Empathy.

Supporting a loved one with avoidant personality disorder (AvPD) can be challenging, but it is also extremely important. Understanding their condition and demonstrating empathy can make a significant difference in their rehabilitation process. In this section, we'll examine why understanding and empathy are important, how to cultivate them, and how they can benefit both you and your loved one.

Why Understanding and Empathy Matter.

Understanding and empathy are vital because they enable you to connect with your loved one on a deeper level and provide the support they need. By understanding the challenges they face and showing empathy for their experiences can help them feel understood, accepted, and less alone in their struggles. This can strengthen your relationship and create a more supportive environment for their recovery.

How to cultivate Understanding and Empathy.

1. **Educate Yourself:** Take the time to learn about AvPD, its symptoms, and how it affects your loved ones' lives. This can give you a better understanding about their experiences and behavior.

2. **Listen without Judgment:** When a loved one wants to talk, listen to them without judgment. Allow them to express their thoughts and emotions without fear of being judged or rejected.

3. **Put Yourself in Their Shoes:** Imagine what it's like to live with AvPD. This can help you connect with their struggles and respond to them with compassion.

4. **Validate Their Feelings:** Acknowledge your loved one's feelings and experiences, even if you don't completely understand them. Validation can assist them feel heard and understood.

5. **Be Patient:** Recovery from AvPD can be a slow process. Be patient with your loved one and don't pressure them to change before they're ready.

6. **Offer Support:** Let your loved one know you're there for them and ready to help in any way you can. This could include listening, providing practical help, or accompanying them to therapy sessions.

Benefits of Understanding and Empathy.

1. **Improved Communication:** Understanding and empathy can help you and your loved one communicate more effectively, making it easier to discuss difficult things.

2. **Stronger Relationship:** Showing understanding and empathy can strengthen your bond with your loved one, creating a more supportive and loving environment for their healing.

3. **Increased Trust:** When your loved one feels understood and empathized with, they are more likely to trust you and open up to you about their experiences.

4. **Reduced stress:** Understanding your loved one's challenges and responding to them with empathy can help to minimize their anxiety and stress.

5. **Increased Self-Awareness:** Cultivating understanding and empathy can also help you become

more self-aware and compassionate toward people in general.

Finally, understanding and empathy are essential in helping friends and relatives who suffer from avoidant personality disorder. By educating yourself, listening without judgment, and providing unconditional support, you can create a more compassionate and supportive environment for your loved one's recovery.

Communication and Validation.

Supporting a loved one with avoidant personality disorder (AvPD) requires effective communication and validation. They help create a safe and understanding environment, creating trust and connection. In this section, we'll take a look at why communication and validation are necessary, how to improve them, and how they can benefit both you and your loved one.

Why Communication and Validation Matter.

Communication is the foundation of any relationship, but it's especially important when caring for someone with AvPD. Clear and empathic communication can make your loved one feel understood and supported, which is essential for their recovery. Validation, on the other side, is the recognition and acceptance of your loved one's feelings and experiences. It can help them feel heard and valued, reducing their feelings of isolation and rejection.

How to Improve Communication and Validation.

1. **Listen Actively:** When your loved one is speaking, give them your complete attention. Listen without interrupting, and show that you're engaged by nodding or making eye contact.

2. **Use Empathetic Language:** Use language that shows empathy and understanding. For instance, instead of saying, "You shouldn't feel that way," try saying, "I can see why you would feel that way."

3. **Ask Open-Ended Questions:** To encourage your loved one to share their thoughts and feelings, ask open-ended questions. This can make them feel more comfortable opening up to you.

4. **Reflect Their Feelings:** Reflecting your loved one's feelings back to them can make them feel understood. For example, you could say, "It sounds like you're feeling extremely anxious about the upcoming event."

5. **Avoid Judgment:** Try not to judge or criticize your loved one's thoughts or feelings. Instead, offer support and understanding.

6. **Validate Their Feelings:** Acknowledge your loved one's feelings and express empathy. You could say "It makes sense that you would feel that way given your past experiences."

7. **Use "I" Statements:** Rather than saying, "You always avoid social situations," say, "I am concerned when I notice you avoiding social situations." This way, you can express your feelings without assigning blame.

8. **Be Patient and Understanding:** Avoidant individuals may have difficulty expressing themselves or need more time to understand information. Be patient and give them enough space to communicate effectively.

9. **Encourage Two-Way Communication:** Create a safe space for open discussion. Encourage your loved one to express their thoughts and feelings, and then respond with empathy and understanding.

10. **Set Clear Expectations:** Be clear about your needs and expectations, and encourage your loved one to do the same. This can help to avoid misconceptions and enhance effective communication.

11. **Seek Professional Help Together:** If communication difficulties persist, consider seeing a therapist or counselor. A mental health expert can advise you on how to improve communication and build your relationship.

Benefits of improved communication and validation.

1. **Improved Relationship:** Effective communication and validation can help you and your loved one build a more supportive and trusting bond.

2. **Reduced Anxiety:** When your loved one feels understood and validated, they may experience less anxiety and stress.

3. **Increased Self-Esteem:** Validation can help raise your loved one's self-esteem and confidence by making them feel more accepted and valuable.

4. **Enhanced Problem-Solving:** Effective communication can lead to better problem-solving since

you and your loved one can work together to overcome difficulties.

5. Increased Emotional Connection: By communicating empathetically and validating your loved one's feelings, you can strengthen your emotional bond with them.

6. Acknowledge Their Struggles: Validate your loved one's experiences by acknowledging the challenges they face. Saying something like, "I can understand how challenging it is for you to attend social events," is one example.

7. Express Empathy: Show empathy by trying to understand your loved one's perspective. You could say, "I can imagine just how difficult that situation must have been for you."

8. Validate their Feelings, Not Necessarily Their Actions: It's crucial to validate your loved one's feelings, even if you disagree with their actions. For example, you could say, "I understand how anxious you are, but I think it would be helpful to try attending the event."

9. Avoid Minimizing Their Feelings: Avoid statements like "It's not a big deal" or "You're overreacting." Instead, support their feelings by expressing, "I understand that this is upsetting for you."

10. **Offer Reassurance:** Let them know that their feelings are valid and that you are there to support them. You could say, "It's okay to feel this way, and I'm here to help you through it."

Finally, communication and validation are essential in helping friends and relatives who suffer from avoidant personality disorder. By improving your communication skills and validating your loved one's feelings, you can create a more supportive and understanding environment, which is important for their recovery.

Encouraging Professional Help.

Encouraging your loved one to seek professional therapy is a vital step in helping them through their journey with avoidant personality disorder. Professional help can provide them with the guidance, support, and tools they need to manage their symptoms and work toward recovery. In this section, we'll examine why professional help is beneficial, how to encourage your loved one to seek it, and how to support them during the process.

Why Professional Help Is Beneficial.

Professional help, such as therapy or counseling, is beneficial for numerous reasons:

1. **Specialized Knowledge:** Mental health practitioners have specialized knowledge and training in the treatment of AvPD. They can provide your loved one with effective strategies and techniques for managing their symptoms.

2. **Supportive environment:** Therapy creates a safe and supportive environment in which your loved one can explore their thoughts, feelings, and behaviors. It can help them gain insight into their condition and build healthy coping mechanisms.

3. **Medication Management:** In some cases, medication may be prescribed to manage AvPD symptoms such as anxiety or depression. A psychiatrist can assess if medication is appropriate and monitor its effectiveness.

4. **Validation and Understanding:** Therapy can help your loved one feel validated and understood, which is especially beneficial for individuals with AvPD who may feel misunderstood or isolated.

How to Encourage Your Loved One to Seek Professional Help.

1. Express your Concern: Start by expressing your concern about your loved one's well-being. Let them know you care about them and want to help them in getting the help they need.

2. Provide Information: Provide information about AvPD and the benefits of professional assistance. You could share books, articles, or websites with accurate and useful information concerning the disorder.

3. Offer to Help: Offer to assist your loved one in finding a therapist or counselor who specializes in AvPD. You can help them with scheduling appointments or accompany them to their first session.

4. Be Supportive: Be supportive your loved one's decision to get help. Encourage them to take the first step while respecting their pace and readiness.

5. Share Your Experience: Tell your loved one about any positive experiences you've had with therapy or counseling. Hearing about your great experiences may assist to reduce their concerns or anxiety about getting treatment.

How to Support Your Loved One When Seeking Professional Help.

1. **Provide Encouragement:** Encourage your loved one to attend therapy sessions and follow through with any recommendations from their mental health professional.

2. **Respect Their Privacy:** Respect your loved one's privacy throughout therapy sessions. Do not pry or ask for details unless they wish to share them with you.

3. **Be Patient:** Recovery from AvPD takes time, and setbacks may occur along the way. Be patient and supportive, and acknowledge any improvement your loved one makes, no matter how small.

4. **Educate Yourself:** Learn about AvPD and its treatment options. This will allow you to better understand what your loved one is going through and how you can best support them.

5. **Take Care of Yourself:** Helping a loved one with AvPD can be difficult. Take care of yourself by getting help from friends, family, or a therapist if needed.

In conclusion, encouraging your loved one to seek professional therapy and supporting them during the process will help them recover from avoidant personality disorder. You may help your loved one take the first step toward a healthier and happier life by encouraging them, offering information, and being supportive.

Taking Care of Yourself as a Support Person.

Supporting a loved one with avoidant personality disorder (AvPD) can be challenging and emotionally draining. Prioritizing your own well-being is essential for your ability to continue providing effective support. In this section, we'll look at why self-care is important, how to practice it, and the benefits it can bring to both you and your loved one.

Why Self-Care is Important.

Self-care is essential for support persons because it prevents burnout, reduces stress, and enhances your ability to provide effective care. It's like an oxygen mask on an airplane- you need to take care of yourself before you can help others. Neglecting your own well-being can lead to exhaustion and resentment, which may negatively impact the relationship with your loved one.

How to Practice Self-Care.

1. **Set Boundaries:** Create boundaries to protect your time and energy. It's okay to say no to additional responsibilities if they interfere with your self-care.

2. **Make Time for Yourself:** Schedule regular time for activities that help you unwind and recharge, such as reading, exercising, or spending time outdoors.

3. **Seek Support:** Don't be afraid to seek help from friends, family, or a therapist. Talking about your experiences and feelings might help you manage stress and gain perspective.

4. **Practice Mindfulness:** Mindfulness techniques, such as meditation or deep breathing, can help you stay present and less anxious.

5. **Live a Healthy Lifestyle:** Eat a balanced diet, exercise regularly, and get plenty of sleep. Physical health is intimately related to mental wellness.

6. **Engage in Hobbies:** Pursue hobbies or activities that bring you joy and fulfillment. This can help you maintain your sense of identity outside of your work as a support person.

Benefits of Self-Care.

1. **Increased Resilience:** Practicing self-care can help you build resilience and cope better with the challenges of supporting a loved one with AvPD.

2. **Improved Mental Health:** Self-care can reduce stress, anxiety, and feelings of overwhelm, resulting in improved mental health and well-being.

3. **Better Relationship with Your Loved One:** By taking care of yourself, you are better equipped to provide efficient support to your loved one, thus strengthening your relationship.

4. **Role Modeling:** By prioritizing self-care, you set a positive example for your loved one and encourage them to prioritize their own well-being.

5. **Enhanced Empathy and Understanding:** Self-care can help you maintain empathy and understanding for your loved one, especially during challenging times.

In conclusion, self-care is essential for support persons of individuals with avoidant personality disorders. Prioritizing your own well-being ensures that you have the energy and resilience to provide effective support for your loved one. Remember that taking care of yourself is not selfish-- it is important for your own health and the well-being of your relationship with your loved one.

CHAPTER TWELVE.

Looking Ahead: Research and future directions.

Current research trends and findings in Looking Ahead.

As we look to the future of research on avoidant personality disorder (AvPD), it is important to consider the current trends and findings that are shaping our understanding of this complex disorder. In this section, we'll explore some of the latest AvPD research trends and findings, as well as how they may affect the future of diagnosis, treatment, and support for individuals with AvPD.

Research Trends in AVPD.

1. **Neurobiological studies:** Recent research has focused on the neurological foundations of AvPD, with brain imaging studies revealing differences in brain structure and function between those with AvPD and healthy controls. These studies suggest that AvPD may

be associated with abnormalities in brain regions involved in emotion regulation and social cognition.

2. Genetic and environmental factors: There is growing evidence that AvPD may have a genetic component, with research indicating that those with a family history of AvPD or other personality disorders are more likely to experience it. Furthermore, research has demonstrated the importance of environmental factors, such as early life experiences, in the development of AvPD.

3. Comorbidity and Overlap with Other Disorders: According to research, AvPD frequently co-occurs with other mental health disorders, such as social anxiety disorder and depression. There is also evidence that AvPD may share some similarities with other personality disorders, such as borderline personality disorder.

4. Treatment Approaches: Recent research has explored the effectiveness of several treatment approaches for AvPD, including as psychotherapy, medications, and alternative therapies. Studies have shown that psychotherapy, particularly cognitive-behavioral therapy (CBT) and schema therapy, can help reduce AvPD symptoms and improve overall functioning.

Research Findings in AvPD.

1. **Cognitive Biases:** Research has identified cognitive biases in people with AvPD, such as a tendency to perceive social situations as more threatening or negative than they are. These cognitive biases may help to explain the avoidance behavior seen in AvPD.

2. **Emotion Regulation:** According to studies, individuals with AvPD may struggle to regulate their emotions, especially in social situations. This may contribute to the interpersonal difficulties and social avoidance observed in AvPD patients.

3. **Social Cognition:** Research has shown that individuals with AvPD may have trouble understanding social signs and interpreting the intentions of others. These deficiencies may contribute to the social isolation and avoidance behavior seen in AvPD.

4. **Treatment outcomes:** Recent research has yielded promising results in the treatment of AvPD, notably with psychotherapy. Studies have found out that, individuals who receive psychotherapy with AvPD generally see considerable changes in their symptoms and overall quality of life.

Future Directions for Research.

1. **Biomarkers:** Additional research is needed to identify specific biological markers that may be related with AvPD. This could help with early detection and treatment of the disorder.

2. **Genetic Studies:** More study is needed to better understand the genetic mechanisms that drive AvPD. Identifying specific genetic markers associated with AvPD could aid in the identification of at-risk individuals and inform targeted interventions.

3. **Treatment Development:** Future research should concentrate on creating and testing new approaches to treatment for AvPD. This could include novel psychotherapeutic techniques as well as the development of medications specifically designed to treat AvPD symptoms.

4. **Longitudinal Studies:** Longitudinal studies are needed to better understand the progression and prognosis of AvPD throughout time. This could help identify factors that influence treatment response and long-term outcomes.

In conclusion, current research trends and findings are providing valuable insights into the underlying mechanisms of AvPD, as well as informing new approaches to diagnosis, treatment, and support for those living with the disorder. We can improve the lives of those suffering from AvPD and advance our understanding of this complex disorder by continuing to build on these findings.

Advocacy and Awareness Efforts.

Advocacy and awareness efforts have a significant impact on the future of research, diagnosis, and treatment for avoidant personality disorder. We can build a more supportive environment for people with AvPD by raising awareness about the disorder, pushing for better access to care, and eliminating stigma. In this section, we'll look at the significance of advocacy and awareness campaigns, as well as how you may become involved in helping people with AvPD.

Why Advocacy and Awareness Efforts Are Important.

1. **Reducing Stigma:** Advocacy and awareness campaigns can help minimize the stigma attached to

AvPD. By raising awareness and acceptance of the illness, we can build a more supportive and inclusive society for those with AvPD.

2. **Improving Access to Care:** Advocacy initiatives can help people with AvPD get better access to mental health services. This involves campaigning for improved insurance coverage and more financing for mental health programs.

3. **Promoting Research:** Raising awareness can assist to spur research into AvPD, resulting in a greater understanding of the illness and more effective treatment options. Increased awareness can also help attract more researchers to the field of AvPD research.

4. **Empowering Individuals:** Advocacy and awareness campaigns can encourage people with AvPD to seek care and support. Individuals with AvPD may be more willing to seek care and support if they realize they are not alone and that options are available to them.

How You Can Get involved.

1. **Educate Yourself:** Learn more about AvPD and its effects on individuals. This will enable you to become a

more effective advocate and increase awareness in your community.

2. **Raise Awareness:** Share AvPD information with your friends, family, and community. This could involve sharing articles, organizing informational events, or sharing your personal experiences with AvPD.

3. **Advocate for Change:** Write to your elected representatives to push for improved mental health care policies. This could involve campaigning for more financing for mental health initiatives or improved insurance coverage for mental health care.

4. **Support Mental Health organizations:** Support organizations committed to raising awareness of AvPD and supporting those affected by the disorder. This could include giving your time or money to these organizations.

5. **Share Your Story:** If you or someone you know has been affected by AvPD, consider sharing your experience. Personal stories can be extremely effective tools for increasing awareness and reducing stigma.

Benefits of advocacy and awareness efforts.

1. **Increased Understanding:** Advocacy and awareness efforts can increase the general public's understanding of AvPD, leading to greater empathy and support for those with the disorder.

2. **Improved Treatment Options:** By promoting research into AvPD, advocacy effort can help improve treatment options for those suffering from the illness. This may lead to improved patient outcomes and more effective treatments.

3. **Reduced Stigma:** By reducing stigma, advocacy and awareness campaigns can make individuals with AvPD feel more comfortable seeking help and support.

4. **Empowerment:** Advocacy and awareness campaigns can empower people with AvPD to take control of their life and seek the help they need.

Finally, advocacy and awareness efforts play an important role in defining the future of AvPD research, diagnosis, and treatment. We can make the environment more supportive for people suffering from this condition by raising awareness, eliminating stigma, and fighting for better access to care. Your involvement in advocacy and awareness campaigns can make a significant difference in the lives of people with AvPD and their families.

Hope for the Future of AvPD. Treatment and support in Looking Ahead: Research and Future Directions for AvPD.

As we look to the future, there is great optimism for advancements in the treatment and support of those suffering from avoidant personality disorder (AvPD). Researchers and mental health experts are constantly striving to increase our understanding of AvPD and create more effective treatment techniques. In this part, we'll examine some of the reasons for hope and what the future might hold for those with AvPD.

Advancements in Treatment Approaches.

1. **Personalized Treatment Plans:** As we have a better understanding of AvPD, treatment approaches become more personalized. This means that treatment programs can be adjusted to each individual's specific needs, leading to more effective outcomes.

2. **Innovative Therapeutic Techniques:** Therapists are exploring innovative therapeutic techniques to help people with AvPD. These could include experiential

therapies like art or music therapy, as well as newer approaches like virtual reality therapy.

3. **Combination Therapies:** Researchers are looking into the effectiveness of combining several treatments for AvPD, such as medication and psychotherapy. These combined treatments may produce better outcomes for some people.

4. **Online and Teletherapy Options:** The advent of teletherapy and online mental health platforms has made therapy more accessible to people with AvPD. This is especially useful for people who have difficulty interacting with others.

Research into Underlying Mechanisms.

1. **Neurobiological Studies:** Advances in neuroscience studies are shedding light on the underlying brain mechanisms of AvPD. This knowledge can help in the development of targeted treatments that address specific neural pathways associated with AvPD.

2. **Genetic Studies:** hereditary research is shedding light on the genetic factors that may contribute to AvPD. This could lead to the development of genetic testing to identify at-risk individuals and guide early intervention strategies.

3. Understanding Trauma and Early Experiences:

Researchers are learning more about how trauma and early life experiences influence the development of AvPD. This understanding can help to guide trauma-informed therapy techniques.

Improvement in Access to Care.

1. Telehealth and Online Resources: Telehealth and online tools have improved access to mental health care for those with AvPD, particularly those living in remote or underserved areas.

2. Community Support Programs: Community-based initiatives and support groups provide vital support to people with AvPD. These programs provide a sense of community and understanding, which can be especially beneficial for people with AvPD who often feel isolated.

Reducing stigma and increasing awareness.

1. Education and advocacy: Efforts to reduce stigma and increase awareness about AvPD are gaining traction. Education and advocacy efforts are helping to clarify myths and misconceptions regarding the disorder leading to increased understanding and acceptance.

2. **Media Representation:** Positive and accurate portrayals of AvPD in the media can help eliminate stigma and increase awareness. Media outlets are increasingly highlighting the stories of individuals with AvPD, which can help raise awareness and foster empathy.

In conclusion, there is much hope for the future of AvPD treatment and support. Advances in treatment techniques, research into underlying causes, improved access to care, and initiatives to reduce stigma and increase awareness all point to a brighter future for those with AvPD. By continuing to support research and advocacy efforts, we can work toward a future where all individuals with AvPD receive the care and support they need to live fulfilling lives.

CONCLUSION.

Embracing Hope and Healing.

Congratulations! You've completed this journey towards overcoming avoidant personality disorder (AvPD). Throughout this book, we've explored the complexities of AvPD, looked at various strategies for managing and overcoming its challenges, and discussed the importance of seeking professional help and creating a supportive environment. As we conclude this book, let us reflect on the progress you have made, and look forward to the future with hope and optimism.

Reflecting on Your Journey.

Think back to when you initially started this journey. Perhaps you were feeling overwhelmed by social situations, struggling to form meaningful connections, or experiencing persistent feelings of inadequacy and self-doubt. You've made significant progress since then. You have learned how to manage your symptoms, taken strides toward healthier relationships, and demonstrated remarkable strength and resilience in the face of difficulties.

Celebrate Your Progress.

-Take a minute to celebrate your progress.

-Acknowledge the challenges you've overcome, no matter how small they may seem.

-Celebrate the moments of courage and vulnerability, the times when you pushed yourself out of your comfort zone, and the moments of connection and growth.

-Each step you've taken has brought you closer to living a life free of the limitations of AvPD.

Embrace Hope for the Future.

As you look ahead, remember that healing is a journey, and it's okay to take it one step at a time. You've already shown that you have the strength and resilience to face the challenges of AvPD. With consistent effort and help, you can continue to grow and thrive.

Keep Your Progress.

It's crucial to continue practicing the coping strategies you've learned and seek help when needed.

Surround yourself with individuals who understand and can assist you along the process. Remember that setbacks are a natural part of the healing process and do not diminish the progress you have made.

The Power of Self-Compassion.

Above all, be gentle and compassionate with yourself.

You deserve to be loved and accepted for who you are.

Practice self-care, do things that make you happy and fulfilled, and remember that your worth is not defined by your challenges or limitations.

Message of Encouragement.

As we conclude this chapter, remember that you are not alone on this journey. There is hope, there is support, and a brighter future ahead. Keep moving forward, believe in yourself, and never underestimate your own strength and determination.

In conclusion, overcoming avoidant personality disorder is a journey that requires courage, perseverance, and self-compassion. You've already taken the first steps toward healing, and while the road ahead may have its challenges, with the right support and mindset, you can continue to move forward and live a fulfilling life. Remember, you are strong, capable, and deserving of a life free from the constraints of AvPD. Embrace the journey, the healing, and the hope for a better future.

30 SELF-REFLECTION QUESTIONS.

Self-reflection is an extremely effective approach for personal growth and overcoming avoidant personality disorder (AvPD). Here are 30 useful self-reflection questions to guide you along your journey:

1. What situations trigger anxiety or avoidance in you?

2. How do you typically respond to these triggers?

3. What beliefs or thoughts are responsible for your avoidant behavior?

4. How does your relationship with others influence your feelings of avoidance?

5. What positive qualities or strengths do you possess?

6. How can you overcome negative self-beliefs and build self-confidence?

7. What small steps can you take to gradually confront your fears?

8. How do you feel when you avoid social situations? How do you feel when you push yourself to participate?

9. What activities or hobbies make you happy and help you feel more confident?

10. How do you practice self-care and improve your emotional well-being?

11. What role does perfectionism play in your avoidant behavior?

12. How can you practice self-compassion and forgiveness for your past mistakes?

13. What are some healthy coping mechanisms you can employ when feeling overwhelmed?

14. How do you set realistic goals for yourself and celebrate your progress?

15. What support systems do you have in place, and how can you strengthen them?

16. How do you deal with criticism or rejection, and how can you improve this?

17. What are some negative thought patterns you should challenge?

18. How can you improve your communication skills and build better relationships?

19. How do you perceive yourself in comparison to others, and how can you cultivate a more positive self-image?

20. What strategies can you employ when struggling with your anxiety in social situations?

21. How do you handle change, and how can you become more adaptable?

22. What are your long-term goals, and how does conquering AvPD align with them?

23. How do you view failure, and how can it be reframed as a learning opportunity?

24. What boundaries do you need to create to protect your emotional well-being?

25. How can you practice mindfulness and be present in the moment?

26. What are some self-reflective practices that speak to you, and how can you incorporate them into your everyday life?

27. How do you define success and track your progress towards it?

28. What affirmations or mantras can help you remain positive and motivated?

29. How can you express your gratitude for the improvements you have made and the support you have received?

30. What advice would you give someone else struggling with AvPD, and how can you apply it to yourself?

Take your time to reflect on these questions and write down your thoughts. Use them as a guide to deepen your understanding of yourself, challenge your beliefs, and take positive steps toward overcoming AvPD.

Made in United States
Troutdale, OR
12/27/2024

27307397R00096